Sovereign ____ove

Bright Ideas for a Better Future

Dr Hannah Jewel McClure

Jewel of Peace

Out there beyond ideas of right doing and wrong doing, there is a field. I'll meet you there.

Mevlana Jalaluddin Rumi

First, the inner revolution. To give love, to give empathy; it is this that will change the world

Vottorio Arrigoni

Contents

About the Author

Hannah began her healing journey in movement and dance. Following this trajectory through to a professional performance career, she there discovered energy therapies. Over eight years, through graduate level study, Hannah explored Ayurvedic, osteopathic and energetic techniques for healing. After several years of private practice, Hannah lectured at university, teaching energy healing, somatics, dance, theatre and movement analysis.

Hannah holds a BFA in Dance from SUNY Brockport, an MA in Dance Anthropology from Roehampton University, and a PhD in Practice as Research from the University of East London. Her doctorate thesis 'Actualising the Contents of the Heart: the practice-based journey of a female Mevlevi semazen' analysed the Mevlevi initiation process through three seasons of performance making.

Hannah's commitment to beauty and healing supports the wellbeing of her students' psycho-spiritual-bodies. She has several academic publications and is delighted to bring forward this new text to bring love to the needs and issues of our moment in time.

www.hannahjewelofpeace.com

Acknowledgements

I would like to thank Michael and Pat Sclater, as well as Vanessa, Nico and Rose Arbuthnott, for their incredible generosity and support in providing space away from my home and worldly duties to write. To my friends and siblings, for their continued encouragement and belief in me, thank you. To Kaiah Miller, for his poignant input and questions in earlier drafts of the writing, I am forever grateful. Without the blessing of Allah, God, Great Spirit, this book would not exist. I give thanks to the plant spirit of tobacco for helping me to speak with love and truth. And I give thanks to our spiritual elders for their incredible generosity in sharing their wisdom. Finally, to Helios, my puppy, for his ever present companionship in the midnight hours of putting pen to paper, I am eternally grateful.

Foreword

Hannah Jewel has the ability to visually paint a picture with the specific use of her words which I find personally incredible. The message within the writing is there to permeate through the consciousness, subtly and yet with great impact. Sitting around the fire with stories from the ancient ones coming back through the oral tradition, I was there in real time in my imagination. The art of storytelling needs reviving, to be brought about again for the teachings to be able to be forthcoming, especially for the benefit of the children to learn the messages of wisdom, inherent within the oral traditions. Earlier this year I watched a programme on The Children's Fire. It showed how the wood was lit and how the fire is shared in many ways, with the continual flame being transported to many places. Carrying and keeping the fire is a tradition that also needs remembering so that we honour the children, who are indeed our future.

Having known Hannah over many years, the depth and breadth of her knowledge in a multitude of specific areas is astounding. Especially with her transformational service through her ritual and bodywork, and much, much more. She also has the ability to stand in a place of total humility and this is a great gift.

When all differing levels and systems are integrated within a whole being peace is the natural outcome. When all parts are accepted and allowed to be as they are in love then the whole has coalesced in total balance. There is much wisdom in this book gathered over many years of experience through Hannah's own journey, which we can all learn from and apply into our own lives.

Being asked to create the cover for the book was an absolute pleasure – the image forming in my imagination before the end of the conversation!

Wishing Hannah every success with her book,

Lyn Marie Whiteman RPP, IPHM, PTP

Part 1

Introduction

That which is delicate must be protected.
That which is resilient has the power to endure.
That which is born of love is reciprocal in kindness.
Hannah Jewel

We must be impeccable with our beginnings.
Bonnie Bainbridge Cohen

The initial conditions of any activity, project or phase render its final shape and outcome. And we are in the initial conditions of wholly new ways of living. As the smallest breeze can completely change the shape of smoke coming from a candle, the attention that we afford to our choices in this moment is of the greatest importance.

This is a book about prophecy, about story, about the epic journey of humanity, and about love. Stories bring us closer, allow us to learn from and imprint one another with the particular grace that divine love has poured into our particular vessel. In this way, we become one, one with the beating heart that we all share. A bigger picture calls to us from across time. And it is these voices from the past/present/future, when put in conversation with the moment of our transition, that will awaken the spark of our collective fire and will power. Our conversations will afford us the grace with which to move forward.

I felt the urge to begin writing in November of 2019. As I began collecting notes, the world began to change around me. As those changes continued I felt a growing impulse to bring through a wider discussion. There are perspectives I carry that I was not seeing in the media, and not hearing most people speak of. I also felt an impulse to shelter, both myself and others. Not to shelter in place, but to provide shelter for the heart, some sense of safety and calm. Over the course of this writing, what has grown most within me is a sense of unity with all beings and with all life on the planet. It is, in truth, from this growing sense of unity that I felt compelled to complete the text. In July of 2021, as I was moving into edits for the final draft, I myself came down with covid. I felt this was serendipitous, as the best writing comes from direct experience. And while I address many other issues within this text, the fact that we are in the midst of a pandemic cannot be ignored. It is in fact a vital ingredient to our catalyst for change.

For those with a practice, hewn over years to a fine point, we may engage this time with a set of legs to lean into. In times of change, be they personal or collective, it is my practices that have carried me through the dark night. My practices have helped me to let go of extraneous thoughts, extra information, and bring me to the presence of this work.

For those lucky enough to have friendship and support, clean water, fresh air, etc. there are many teachings to be learned. In the West, as a people who largely go uninitiated through life, the experience of facing our potential death affords us a stepping stone to our deepest truth. A deep compassion emerges for those whose Machiavellian needs are greater than ours, not by ideology but by experience itself. For one thing is certain: we are, as one human family, moving through our transition together. There is not a single person on this planet who has not been touched or affected in some way by the changes of the last two years. And while the changes may express differently from region to region, we can now agree that we all have something to share in common.

As we navigate our present ship, I find standing in a place of non-judgement to be essential. It may be a long time before the complete truth of circumstances comes out, and even then we may never agree on it. In truth, we don't have to fully agree or come to some form of global consensus – because to do so would squash the inborn rights of every human to make sense of the world for themselves. Each one of us is a universe unto their own. And it is the touching of one universe to another where fresh life and innovation are born. We do in truth need each other to complete the pattern of our new normal, or our new Earth.

Processes of maturation are taking place within our consciousness. We are facing our fears together. And one of the challenges we face as a species is how: How do we come together? How do we address the global whole while still honouring the individual and their freedoms, their choices? What do unity and peace actually look like? And if we take responsibility for that peace, how do we desire to shape it?

We are the hope of the future. We are the ones who can resolve the past. We are the ones who are living, right now, thus we are the ones who can and must necessarily do something about the situation we find ourselves in.

A rich and diverse tapestry of solutions awaits us. The more we can localise and live fully, joining our hearts with every being on the planet, the more colourful and abundant our tapestry will be. As we slow down, we may rest and reconfigure, we may learn to sing again, to dance in circles and community. If we choose, we can participate in a collective enlivening of our hearts. If we can imagine such a space of beauty, if we can perceive it, in that moment it becomes real. More real than anything else.

What Is Sovereignty and Why Is it Important?

Sovereignty is a concept with layers. A sovereign nation is one ruled by a sovereign, one who reigns over the subjects of the nation in, hopefully, a dutiful and kind capacity. A nation that is independent from other nations, in charge of its own resources, in possession of its own culture. A nation that is unified by the fact that all of its inhabitants dwell within one idea of who they are, and this idea is in fact the most important defining factor of their personhood. The sovereign, or leader, makes decisions that benefit the subjects, money is transferred from subject to sovereign, and the sovereign distributes the money equally and fairly so that all are in possession of the accoutrements of civilisation. The age of empires and before that the age of kings relied on the concept of a sovereign who was sanctified by God in order to fairly place, or in some cases – manipulate, the subjects into submission. And because the subjects were able to pursue ease, learning and culture from within this conceptual structure, they readily agreed. So attractive was the concept that over time, as the costs of civilisation slowly began to outweigh the benefits, we clung to the overriding machinations. We are now at a point where old concepts of sovereignty have reached their limit. And we, as individuals who together form a global human collective, may now redefine it so that life may be created afresh and lived with fullness of purpose and health.

Right now the term 'sovereignty' is being redefined in different ways. Here in the UK, some are using the term to denote independence from any governing or government structure. Declaring sovereignty in this manner can be done legally, and offers a person status as their own nation. However, such a move effectively isolates one from the rest of society, as they can no longer use the roads, hospitals, schools or any other public services. Others relate the term directly to our Queen and the royal family. In this case the term is laden with its historical and imperial ties. I am asking us to consider the term on a spiritual level. From a spiritual perspective, every man on this Earth is king and every woman is queen – of their own heart. They alone bear the weight of their heart's decisions and the impact this will have on others. And none can take this sovereignty away. Or deny it its voice and existence. As we collectively inverse the idea of a monarchy, we may re-cognise[1] sovereignty as the royal, divine, guardianship and care of an individual over themselves.

Because sovereignty enfolds other concepts such as free will, divine will, destiny and fate within it, it becomes a perennial turning point. Equally, sovereignty reflects our ability, or lack thereof, to take basic care of ourselves. At this moment it is critical that we reclaim food sovereignty, water sovereignty, energy and housing sovereignty and our freedom of movement. Like life, like love, like God, sovereignty is something we must turn toward and embrace at some point. And because sovereignty is so important, I bring it forward as a foundational concept to this text.

One of the central questions we as a species are working out right now is, 'Where do the individual and collective meet?'. As a network of sovereign beings, how do we desire to live and be together? The more we dare to let go of our current structures, the more we will find ourselves knee deep in resolving ways of mutual cooperation.

To be sovereign may be to stand in alignment with the essence of beauty and freedom in itself. To be sovereign may be to recognise the power and wholeness of every 'other' while knowing your own root. For me, to be sovereign is to know oneself and to act from the centre of that knowledge with love, courage and trust.

What Is Love and Why Is it Important?

There are many kinds of love. In the English language we have only one word for all of them. In Greek and Turkish, however, multiple words exist. We are all familiar with romantic love and its distinct passions. Perhaps stronger is familial love, between a parent and child, sibling, aunts, uncles, cousins. There is the love of friendship, unique and precious in its own right. A love for nature and creation imbues our very breath and essence if we allow it to. And then there is the divine unity – known as *samadhi* in India and related to the experience of death in Sufi mysticism[2]. Each of these early, or earthly loves, has

---

1 I use a hyphen here to present recognition as a re-cognisation, or mental re-wiring of a way of perceiving or thinking.

2 There are several distinct forms of samadhi, each relating to deeper and deeper states of ultimate union. Likewise, there are several distinctions within Sufism relating to a dissolution of self in ever-increasing modes. What we see with our earthly senses is but a sprout of the vast root system existent in the more subtle spheres.

the capacity to lead us back to the divine, to God, to the source of all forms of life, love and existence. And it is to the source, that 'love supreme', that I direct our attention.

One of the most precious gifts of humanity is the power of our heart. In spiritual teachings from across traditions, we are born on this Earth to work through our personal karma, to learn lessons, but more importantly we are born to connect our soul to the heart of God. It is our hearts that allow us to melt into that connection. Such a connection is far beyond the mind, though the mind can be a tool to either help or hinder us on our path. Such a connection is far beyond the senses and the emotions they are part of. Such a love cannot be described in language, but it can be known by experience. Mevlana Jalaluddin Rumi, figurehead of the Mevlevi Order of Sufis, writes 'A life lived without love is of no account. Don't ask yourself what kind of love you should seek, spiritual or material, divine or mundane, Eastern or Western. Divisions only lead to more divisions. Love has no labels, no definitions'[3]. In the passage Rumi speaks of embracing all forms of love, because they open the heart spark. What kindles the fire can help it to grow. And when we are ready, we begin to mature our understanding of love.

As we look for solutions to our present transitions, let us not confuse the power of our heart with our lower desires. As we elevate ourselves to sovereign kings and queens of our own hearts, let us focus the power of our hearts toward the ultimate. For, in my experience, nothing less will suffice to move us collectively beyond the karmic cycles[4] we are witness to and part of.

Related to Sovereignty and Love Is the Concept of Grace

There is a river flowing from the heart of the universe, the heart of God, the heart of creation, and it is a river of grace. In his/her desire to know themselves, the impulse that we call God – the seed of love before it is manifest or in motion, the seed of all existence undulated this desire. A fold was made in the void, and from it came vibration: movement and sound. And the nature of

---

3 Where possible I have quoted directly from the written works of Rumi. Many of Rumi's sayings have been translated multiple times and it is not possible to trace the original passage.

4 Karma is a concept from Hinduism/Vedanta which speaks to the causality of the lessons we each have to learn. Personal karma can be carried across lives, and it can take time to work itself out. Collective karma works itself out even more slowly. The issues we are attending to now may be the result of many generations of choices in the causal manner.

this desire is circular, for it wants to come back to itself in recognition. And for this desire to move back unto itself, there had to be imprinted in the original vibration a moment of choice. And as love unfurled from its heart the jewelled capacity for choice, with it came the presence and care that would be required to enact an ever-repeating undulation home. This jewel can be known as the human condition. This presence we know and feel as grace.

For me, sovereignty and grace are linked in a profound way, much like a keyhole and key. For it is a moment of sovereignty, the moment that we choose to live fully within love above all else, and it is an absolute grace, which we depend upon, to make such a choice.

To open this relationship further, we can recognise that all possibilities are latent within the human condition. We may call them good or evil, right or wrong, but in actuality they are there as a contrast so that action may take place. Action, friction, creation. Without polarities, the only potential is still-ness. And stillness is not a moment of choice, but rather the presence behind that choice. This life we live, in all of its dimensions of plausibility, is one where action is necessitated – creation is therefore the foundation. And with all the possibilities that we may choose, on our way to choosing love, only grace will fully serve. So from the heart of love, a grace that is vast enough to enfold within it complete and total forgiveness, the heights of ecstasy, and the dregs of despair was born. We are gifted a grace so pure that it will spark hope from the touchstone of the heart – and with even the most subtle of direction, point that movement home. Without grace we might each remain a slave to the weight of our own creations. But with grace, the wings of the heart lift into flight.

As well as sovereignty and love, concepts covered in this writing include unity, leadership, beauty, interdependence, reciprocity and care. The role of the feminine and her rise out of subjugation and oppression is part of the writing. Prophecy is sprinkled throughout, as well as legend and mythology, for these speak to the choices we have before us. The guidance of elders and of thought leaders in our current time are included. Together these elements weave a pattern with many layers.

The first part of the text is structured as a discourse on seven levels. I chose seven for the manifold ways seven can act as a structure of transformation. There are, for instance, seven energy centres along the human spine – known as chakras in the Hindu/Vedic philosophies. There are seven vices and seven virtues in Western/Christianised philosophies. And seven generations is the number of cycles in which genetic information is active in a single body.

Every spiritual tradition states that to solve a problem on one level one must look from a higher plane, from above that level, in order to see clearly. And there are multiple problems on the table right now. A key point of this book is, through critique and love, to encourage momentum around a different conversation. When we broaden our perspectives, we may perceive viewpoints that allow us to address each of our problems more fully and perhaps with more kindness and compassion. Because I personally have had enough of our various problems. They have gone on for too many generations. And if our sorrows are from war, famine, displacement or pandemic does it make them more or less real? I ask us to look with sobriety at a bigger constellation of issues and concerns. Perhaps there are other alternatives to our habitual military style responses. Perhaps there are new or unheard voices that need to be brought forward in order to reach sound, grounded decisions. Perhaps there is wisdom in the stories of our spiritual elders.

This is a time when we can see ourselves clearly as human beings. Right now we can see our addiction to convenience, our structures and our stories. And through fresh sight, we may liberate ourselves into something better. Dr Carolyn Myss, author and healer, teaches, 'That which remains hidden will maneuver us in the dark' (1996). And as many things have recently come to public light, many more are yet to come forward from the depths of our subconscious. Because the truth is that we were not shifting. In the face of climate devastation, rising mental health issues and continued slavery, we were not able to stop the rhythms of our consumption. Yet there is a bigger truth. Which is that we have the potential to create true joy and abundance for all of us, every one. We have the potential to live simply and in harmony with each other. And we have the potential to live in a state of wonder.

If there is one common denominator at the bottom of our moment, it is the way we value life. Like other big, perennial questions, how we value life is foundational to how we live it. And there is not one right answer. Because what is protective for one person may be handicapping for another. What is healing to one person may not be the right solution for another. But if we can come to a collective realisation that we value the opportunity for life, as a unique phenomenon of this blessed Earth, that is a rather big collective leap.

This book opens a pathway for the heart and soul. It asks us to consider the present moment in time from broader perspectives – ones that include the rise and fall of civilisations, our previous shamanic cultures and new possibilities for the future. Through sovereignty, we can foster a deep connection to love, which in turn opens bright ideas. Or for others, a deep connection to love may allow them to embrace sovereignty, and from that place their bright star is born.

The point of this writing is not to preach for any specific set of actions or beliefs. In this writing I address you, as your own sovereign beings, and ask you to participate in this conversation from the truth of your own precious, significant and valuable lives. Your inner truth brings unique gifts to our collective solution making process.

Biographical context

Finally, a little about the person whose heart and thoughts you will be reading from throughout the text. I grew up in California, the daughter of a military father and a stay-at-home mom. My mom was educated, loved the arts, and did so much to foster an appreciation of life, beauty and good thinking in me. My father was a hard worker, and after he left the military he often took on two or more jobs at once in order to provide for us. My parents were aligned with contemporary Christianity, which in America can be rather fundamentalist in its nature. So in addition to the good things I inherited from my family, I was also fed large doses of prejudice, unhealthy behaviours and confusion.

As a very young child I knew in the core of my being that the world was different than what I saw at home. And by the age of 11, I had read the Bible cover to cover twice. By the age of 14, I had begun researching and reading from every tradition I could find. As I spread my teenage wings through California, I met people of every kind. All of this helped greatly to put my childhood into context and open new vistas. I am so thankful to the many New Age hippies who opened my eyes enough to start seeking deeper truth. I am so thankful to the First Nations people who patiently taught me the ways of the Earth. And I am truly thankful to the storytellers, anthropologists and elders who have recorded their teachings in books of every kind.

In addition to my early experiences, I find in my life many visions, dreams and incredible people. Somehow, we are led to those who will help shape our thinking, our actions and our lives in just the way our hearts are leading. My immersion in the Sufi path has opened vistas to knowledge and love which I could not have previously imagined. A deep recognition of all ancient paths to truth and love is thus woven into my fabric.

For many years I have known that I will write books. In 2015 I received in a vision an image of five books that I was to write. In March of 2020, as lockdown became enforced across the UK, I, like many others, had many feelings and musings to consider. And even though I had previous information about what was to come, through spiritual and material forms, it still caught me off guard. I needed to respond, and to do that I brought the knowledge which had been simmering in me for 20 years to the task.

Though I have been, and am, an academic, I have written the book in the simplest way possible. My aim is to open conversations between us, conversations that have hope, the heart and love woven through them. Following the Dalai Lama and Mahatma Gandhi, I do believe that when a certain percentage of the population is steadily practising meditation and nonviolence, we will see more change in one generation than we have in the previous four (Bader, 2012; Yogananda, 2007). We are not far away.

We are in an incredible time, where we have an opportunity to shape the way we live our lives in a completely new fashion. By necessity, new forms of healthcare, education, housing and food production will come into being. This could, in fact, be a bountiful time. And it is toward this potentiality that I direct our attention. For how we get there is as important as what we birth. What, from our previous civilisations and knowledges, will we keep in the basket? What will we let go of?

All change is momentous. And the changes that we are face in our particular lifetimes are the ones we get to work with. In embracing change, we will find ourselves to be the necessary creators of solutions. When we, as individuals who are part of a whole, are studious with our own hearts, we may indeed birth solutions that impact the whole for the better, because they will be filled with inner unity and love and thus become a thread of peace in the fabric of our existence.

Chapter One

Seven Levels: Levels One to Three

Seven is a number of manifestation. It is also a number representing forgiveness. There are seven virtues and there are seven vices. An infinite plateau spreads out across the top of number 7, and a root descends infinitely down. It is said in the Quran, the sacred text of Islam, that each line carries seven levels of meaning. Your whole life you may read the Quran, and only when a new layer is ready to be perceived within you does that level of meaning make itself known. The deep metaphysical meanings are not often conveyed via language, but by vibration, colour, light and sound. For this reason the Quran is sung. Thus further layers of perception may imbue within us as we receive through other senses. In the making of meaning and symbolism, physical and metaphysical intertwine. And this is a reflection of the human body. For we are not neatly divided bodies, minds and spirits. We are psycho-spiritual-bodies who exist across dimensions of knowing and experience. For each person, further dimensions open as and when we are ready for them. So we are utilising seven as a construct for seeing.

Related to seven are maps of the human system from India and its Vedic tradition. In this system there are over 250 maps of the human energy system that I am aware of[1]. A most basic map is that of the seven chakras, or metaphysical centres, along the spine. These are centres where energy converges. In four of the seven centres there is a correlating nerve plexus. The cervical nerve plexus relates to the fifth centre, the brachial to the fourth, the lumbar to the second and the sacral to the first. Organs and tissues are related to each of the seven centres, as well as meridians and elemental qualities.

---

1 The maps I utilise are from a system called Polarity Therapy (Stone, 1986). It is the merging of osteopathic and Ayurvedic knowledges. In this way the metaphysics of the ancient texts are brought forward. Pure Ayurveda is an even more vast and ancient knowledge. Contemporary training covers about one-sixth of the knowledge base. It may be possible, in the future, to recover much of the lost knowledge through a reinvigorated study of the ancient texts in full.

In this chapter we move through the first three centres. In terms of a journey, it is in the first three centres that the most dense vibrations, discussions and issues are encountered. I encourage us to take heart at the start of the journey. To get to the mountain top we start at the base. We may walk through broad rivers, narrow streams and steep valleys and climb some rock cliffs. In every area, be it fertile or dry, difficult or a blessing, we have a chance to come face to face with our patterns of belief. In this we can choose to interact with our present transitions from a place of agency. For we are at the birth of a new and emerging state of human consciousness. From the vista of the first three centres we are at an equally tragic and beautiful moment, both letting go and emerging. This moment requires courage and conviction. And in the end we each can only trust and act on the direction our own sovereign heart chooses. We are part of a bigger plan. And no matter how frightening it may seem, we can trust that bigger plan. Through trust, faith and hope, we might yet connect and empower our collective heart. Together we can bring ourselves into a more beautiful world than we have so far dared to imagine.

Level One: Health and Symbiosis

The first chakra is located at the base of the spine. It rests between the lower halves of the pelvis, in the soft tissues there. Its colour is red and it is associated with the element of earth. The areas of food, shelter and safety predominate. How we relate to earth, how we adapt to her cycles and moods, how we steward and how we care for each other are a first and primary concern.

At the first level, ideas of health and disease, contagion and adaptation can be addressed. Our collective fear of mortality also comes up. From both spiritual and scientific perspectives, we have found ourselves in a real predicament. My heart sees that our way through is to look with clear eyes, in acceptance of all that we see. As we begin to observe issues of the lower chakra centres, we can move that seeing into the space of the heart. For the heart centre is able to burn through the sludge. In the still place at the centre of the fire, natural solutions reveal themselves from within. Fire, while predominantly related to the third centre, is actually present in multiple chakra centres: in the first centre it is part of the fire of digestion (through extraction and elimination); in the third of transformation, via willpower; in the fourth, within the crucible of the heart; and; in the sixth, through vision. So at the first centre let us look at what we cannot receive nourishment from. For the level of a problem is not where the level of the solution resides. To solve a predicament, we must move into other realms of thinking, feeling and knowing to find the cure. As we look at the issues of the first level, know that solutions will arise as we rise. Transmutation is a process.

Pandemic, famine and climate crisis may be part of naturally occurring cycles; however, they are more likely the effects of overconsumption and neglect. It is truly both. The Earth moves in geological time, and we have had ice ages, tropical ages and ages of desertification. The movement of comets, human impact on land, and the inner movements of the Earth all play a part. We are at a juncture once again. And this time we cannot ignore the parts of our natures that would take more than they give and neglect to ensure resilience for the future. Because of increased floods, fires and storms we must now adapt. The way of life we have created, in the age of civilisations, is no longer going to support us. We may choose to believe in a doomsday or we may choose to rise to an opportunity. A doomsday is certainly possible. And so is an incredibly bountiful future.

In the next section we look at contagion and disease. It was Louis Pasteur, who in developing his theory of germs, found that the ground conditions of the host played a much larger part in the regaining of health than treatment of the germs themselves. We find a similar principle in Ayurveda, which works to address the ground conditions of the digestive system so that the body has resilience to fight off germs itself. In Chinese medicine we see a similar approach again, where illness is treated as an imbalance. To treat the illness it is necessary to restore the initial balance of the whole person. The body then has the resources it needs to address the illness in its own way. We go to the root of the problem, not by pacifying symptoms, but by looking at the imbalances underneath.

From Disease to Health

We are living in a paradigm where we take more from the body than we give it. We are in a paradigm where stress is pacified not by going to the root conditions, but through distraction and consumption. We have been pushing too hard for too long, abusing the body rather than building its resilience. Such a way of living can only result in disease.

Viruses are part of human evolution. We exist as ecological systems embedded within greater systems. We are made up of trillions of organisms which are alive, which eat, release energy, produce waste, and may even share feeling and emotion with us. Viruses enter our system as we move within the natural world, and when handled well, they help us to adapt to ever changing shifts in our environment. As our lives have slowly become removed from nature, viruses and bacteria have become problematic for us. Is this the fault of the virus or an imbalance in our ground conditions? Without natural water, pure air, soil and earth next to our skin, our ability to adapt has become sluggish. We have thus arrived at a moment when, rather than welcoming viruses as a natural part of the immune response to life, we have become afraid of them. They take our time, reduce our productivity, impinge upon our social lives – and we don't like this much. We have become accustomed to ideas of dominion and self-importance. What if we could shift these basic assertions to befriend the natural world and all of its organisms? What if we could accept and flow with discomfort as a natural and necessary part of our very survival?

To address coronavirus itself we may look to the ways we have responded to show us where our underlying imbalances are. For while many of the measures are helpful in preventing contagion, others tip the balance and lead to further disease.

The way bacteria and viruses are treated in an allopathic system has been adopted *en masse*. In this system a fever, which is a symptom, is alleviated so that we are not uncomfortable. Fever, however, burns bacteria up. A fever only reaches the point of disruption when it exceeds a very high threshold – typically 103 degrees Fahrenheit or 39.4 degrees Celsius. Up until this threshold a fever is serving us, as part of a resilient system that responds to contagion through fire. If we were taught to manage our fever, to watch it and care for it, we would empower ourselves in managing our own healthcare. Equally, we approach germs, or living micro-organisms, as something to kill. Germs may actually serve the purpose of testing our body's reserves to ensure we have created enough. By responding to a small amount of germs, the body is encouraged to check on its resources and to bring them up to an optimal level. These resources include things such as white t-cells – which eat bacteria; b-cells – which respond to antigens; mineral levels – which cause the cells to fire and communicate; and oxygen levels – which allow for movement of nourishment across cell walls. When we kill germs we actually destabilise our natural response. For example, alcohol kills not only germs on the skin but also micro-organisms that fight the germs. In trying to sanitise, we actually create a ground for every kind of disease to flourish in. If we were to provide water and natural soap for handwashing we would quickly come into awareness of how much water we use, and how necessary it is for life. Health could not help but be recognised as a symbiotic flourishing: we care for the water, and it helps us to care for each other.

Another way we have responded is through the use of social distancing. This has proven to be effective, but not without harmful side effects. And the harm may stem from an imbalance in the way distancing has been enforced. Even to write the word enforced moves counter to encouraging a health response from my own body. The way we have coerced each other, via fear, into distance is a virus itself. Fear lowers the immune system, just as stress does. A military enforcement creates further fear. A curfew does not stop the spread of contagion in and of itself. A wedding is not more likely to spread contagion than a school classroom. The way we have responded is soaked in the ways of thinking that contributed to the ground conditions. We might safely respect each other without fear, while offering help and care where we are able to. For the truth is we are one body just as we are one heart. The water we drink has already passed through the systems of others, and it is filled with the pharmaceutical drugs they have taken, the hormones they have taken, and the acids and peptides released as waste from their stress responses. To truly address contagion we must address what we are putting into our bodies in the first place. Only from the root will we effectively make use of measures such as distancing.

A distortion is present in our thinking. We continue to be willing to ingest harmful substances, even though we cannot digest them. This includes chemical, additive and preservative substances as well as medical and hormonal ones. Much of the food we eat is filled with bleached, refined sugar and corn syrup, which act as poisons to our tissues and blood. We are able to justify isolation for some, and not for others, based on ideas of incorruptibility afforded through the introduction of foreign substances to the body. Is this not dissimilar to justifying safety, shelter and warmth for some and not for others, based on ideas of entitlement? How are we going to unravel ourselves?

I have come down with covid. As I lay in the bed, drifting in and out of consciousness, I move fluidly between the dream and waking worlds. I cannot come fully to the waking world, for there is too much pain there. I cannot witness it, cannot feel it. But when I go inward I am able to witness, able to see. In the centre of my being, where I am connected to the heart of love, the fortitude comes to face the darkness all around me. It is time of the ending of our karmas. It is the time of releasing all that we have carried. And it is my time to surrender at ever greater thresholds. Illness moves into the body and occupies the grooves left by previous illness. It fills the ruts and the ditches that have worn in over a lifetime of unknowing. As the virus does so, I have an opportunity. To see what I could not see. To bring to awareness the dregs in the ditches of my body memory, the stored emotion there and the trauma of previous generations. With loving awareness now I see you. I thank you and I release you. I am thankful to release you. I am thankful for this illness. And then again, deeper grooves come. Again and again. It goes like this day after day. Layer after layer. And slowly I begin to realise the depth of letting go we are asked to do in this transition. Every one of us is having this cleanse. We are in it together. And I pray for good friends to be present to life with me. That we may surrender together. Deep unravelling comes little by little. Slow down little one. I am thankful for this space. (August 2021)

Liz Hoskins, founder and director of The Gaia Foundation, asks us to consider 'What is at the heart of the paradigm shift required of us?'. She postulates that a connection to nature and to each other underpins our ability to let go of the old and bring in something better. She states, 'It takes time to decolonise our minds and to experience ourselves as participants with the community of life around us, so that our actions are enhancing to all of life' (Hoskins, 2017) We may, very soon, begin to define health differently. For me, health now includes balance, resilience, safety, fresh air, clean water, warmth, shelter, healthy food, companionship, connection, music, movement, expression and the arts, as well as a sense of value, appreciation for the sacred gift of our lives and a shared sacred purpose in serving each other to evolve and to steward the earth. Health may be measured by its fruits, just as illness may be measured by its symptoms. Both are nourished at the root. And we are the ones who can cultivate the soil of our body, environment and spirit so that health is both possible and a lived reality. For all of us.

In looking at the coronavirus itself we are able to look at how we deal with virus and contagion at root levels. Our ideas of health may expand to include many good and beautiful things. As they do, ground conditions which allow things like war, abuse and slavery to root will slowly change. The soil of our consciousness can be truly nourished. But before we get to how to do that, let us look at the soil beneath our feet.

Food Sovereignty
Food sovereignty is a term that embraces the right and responsibility of each individual to clean water, fertile ground, seeds and the time and knowledge to grow their food. Essential to survival, or our ability to exist and have health, is a regular supply of fresh quality food. The reason such a concept is needed is that we have, since the Second World War, given up our rights and responsibil-

ities for producing our own food. To return to balance, we now need to reclaim sovereignty surrounding food.

Dr Vandana Shiva is an activist for women's rights and climate rights in India. She is a physicist by learning and travels globally to educate the public on issues of food sovereignty and farming. While Shiva has been criticised by some, many others applaud her efforts. She is not a perfect human being, rather she is a human being of conviction. Shiva acts as an advisor on food and farming issues to the legislative process in India. Likewise, many individual farmers have been helped by her work. The way Shiva blends empowerment for women, regenerative agriculture and the rights of both women and farmers is unique. Shiva views food sovereignty as the first and most vital step toward individual sovereignty.

Intrinsic to Shiva's concepts of food and human sovereignty are notions of reciprocity and care. Reciprocity is imbued with a recognition that humans are part of a larger whole. That we are organisms within nested ecosystems – and just as our bodies host a huge number of organisms, we are hosted by the planet. We are generously given space to live by the other animals and beings who live here. We may reframe our ideas of both health and food to include reciprocity at their foundation. Rather than view ourselves as parasites upon the planet, we may choose instead to view ourselves as sacred stewards. Sacred sovereign stewards.

In relation to first chakra issues of food, shelter, safety and disease, Shiva brings focus to a quiet democide taking place through the use of pesticides and GMOs, as well as the laws that protect and enforce such use. She writes:

Both the organic movement – toward chemical-free, pesticide free, GMO-free farming – as well as the environmental movement – against climate change – are trying to create a poison-free world. The imperative to spread poisons is not an ecological imperative for how nature works, nor is it a socio-economic imperative for creating thriving economies. Rather, it is only an imperative for corporate profits… There are poison-free ways of farming that are not only possible but successful. Breaking out of the poison cycle is crucial to protecting both our health and our biodiversity. (2016)

Shiva's work is not only to educate, but to actively empower. She brings a voice that others may follow, a voice that exists within India and can benefit from growth. For example, cooperatives in India are leading the way in the production of goods, re-wilding of ecosystems and empowerment of women all at the same time. Where water no longer runs, aloes and water-retaining plants have been introduced in large numbers. Growing under existing trees, the aloes and succulents keep water in the soil. Trees benefit, extending their roots and branches, and aloes proliferate. After just a decade, an entire region may be thriving enough that farming as well as life becomes easier (Shiva, 1988; Mumford, 2016).

With our hands in the soil, we encounter micro-organisms that fortify and stabilise our immune response. With our hands in the soil, we hear the voice of the land. With our hands in the soil, reciprocity and sovereignty become concepts that are more than ideas. They become lived realities which contribute to balance and resilience.

Level Two: Power and Control

The second chakra is centred in the pelvis, sacrum and reproductive organs. There is a nerve plexus here which brings the whole of the lumbar spine and sacrum into refined, continual communication. This centre has everything to do with power, money and sexuality. Its colour is orange and the associated element is water. Where the first chakra allows us to face our fears, the second chakra allows us to feel the emotion of all that we face. How we relate to power, authority and exchange are central concerns in this centre. If we look with a broad and curious eye, we will notice that the last several centuries have seen issues of the second chakra played out at the forefront.

Extinction

Moving from food to power, issues of potential extinction move from rights to access (to water, shelter, community etc) to rights of self-governance. If food and health sovereignty are to be fully reclaimed, the sovereignty of an individual or group to make decisions regarding their methods of governance and peace also need to be in place.

Noam Chomsky is an author, speaker and thinker who has throughout his career questioned major world events for a deeper significance. He is a staunch advocate of democracy and the power of people to organise. His main concerns, from my point of view, are the freedom of civil society and the health of its members. Chomsky argues that contagion is actually the least of our current worries, and that focus on it may pull us away from deeper issues that desperately need addressing (2020). According to Chomsky, as well as other thinkers, we as humans are at the brink of possible extinction[2]. For Chomsky, issues of nuclear armament and climate crisis are two of the major factors contributing to our growing challenge of our survival (2021a). We must first have arable land to grow food on, and to be free from the threat of nuclear missiles if we wish to be successful with the creation of new lifestyles and habitats.

In his thoughts on the climate crisis Chomsky does not focus on whether climate change is man-made or not, but argues that it is observably happening and that if we do not attend to it, we will suffer greatly (2021b). His view is corroborated by indigenous elders the world over. It is several decades ago that the North American Indigenous Elders began to speak to us, their white brothers and sisters, *en masse*. As a deep redress to climate change and the causes which created it, the Hopi Elders have shared what has become a now well-known prophecy:

'You have been telling the people that this is the eleventh hour,
Now you must go back and tell them that this is the hour.
And there are things to be considered…
Where are you living?
What are you doing?
What are your relationships?
Where is your water?
Know your garden.
It is time to speak your truth.
Create your community.
Be good to each other.
And do not look outside yourself for the leader.

This could be a good time!
There is a river flowing now very fast.
It is so great and swift that there are those who will be afraid.
They will try to hold on to the shore.
They will feel they are torn apart and will suffer greatly.

---

2 Among indigenous oral traditions (Cameron, 1981; Banyacya, 1985; Looking Horse, 2010; etc.), as well as spiritual elders from the East (Yogananda, 2007) and thinkers on ecology (Shiva, 1988, 2016; Chomsky, 2021a,b etc.), we are facing the sixth possible extinction. Extinction has occurred previously and it is within our collective memory. Because we have lost the traditional knowledge that would help us to survive such a cataclysm, we are floundering. We may recover our knowledges however. And at the least, we may recover our willpower to see us through.

Know the river has its destination.
The elders say we must let go of the shore, push off into the middle the river,
Keep our eyes open and our heads above water.
See who is in there with you and celebrate.
At this time in history, we are to take nothing personally, least of all ourselves.
For the moment that we do, our spiritual growth and journey comes to a halt.

The time for the lone wolf is over. Gather yourselves!
Banish the word struggle from your attitude and your vocabulary.
All that we do now must be done in a sacred manner and in celebration.'
The Elders of the Hopi Nation (2020)

The climate crisis may well be the defining issue that causes us to address our relationships and the ground conditions of our thinking. For our ability to shelter, feed and clothe ourselves is utterly dependent upon our relationships to each other and our environments. Already, extinction via starvation and exposure are becoming realities for many. Already, many are displaced. Right now, there are millions worldwide without clean water or clean air. Returning to Chomsky, he is a proponent of grassroots movements, or solutions by local people specific to the particulars of their environs. Chomsky also believes in the power of conversation and of democratic process. It is vital that we openly discuss all of the issues on the table, and that we welcome a diverse range of perspectives. It is equally vital that we learn how to govern ourselves within structures of peace. While I personally feel that the structures of the present will not solve the issues we face, they may be of help in the transition, according to the hearts of the people within those structures. We each have the power to influence the life we find ourselves in. And officials are people too. As people, they may choose to be a vital part of community-based solutions, and may play a positive role if they choose. Local solutions abound, though they are not often what we see in the media. Right now, children in Africa are creating solar power and electricity for their villages with salvaged parts and trash. Right now, in unused urban lots across America and much of the world, people are already planting community gardens. Right now, across the world, parents are gathering together to create solutions for schooling their children. People are choosing to travel by boat rather than air where possible. And our solutions will grow. Humans act out of necessity. And as our compassion grows, we will bond together more easily.

In his thoughts on potential nuclear fallout, Chomsky argues that it is a threat much greater than we can conceive of. While the Cold War may have come and gone, there are hundreds of active warheads all over the world. And the culprits that may eventually utilise these missiles may not be those of developing nations. It is rather the leaders of the Western world we must concern ourselves with. For Western psychology is reactionary and abrupt. Our cavalier use of force and our mindset of domination may be the biggest threat we face (2020).

Deeply related to both concerns of climate change and nuclear fallout are indigenous prophecies speaking to directly to our current moment. One of these is encoded in petroglyph on a sacred and protected rock face in the Dakota regions. I have seen a similar glyph, on another rock face in the heart of the Southwest.

In 2017, as part of a trip across Arizona and New Mexico, I went into the desert where the Navajo reside.

On a cliff face, where red stone rises high under the baking sun, where plateaus strut out of the earth reaching into expansive starry nights, where long forgotten rivers which have now vanished carved the spaces where life once teemed, messages remain for us to now read. Messages created for us. Messages of warning and of hope.

I walk on the tourist path to the rock cliff face. There are signs saying, please don't touch, please don't leave offerings and gifts, please just witness and respect. And so we do, my children and I. My daughter immediately points out the prolific growth of datura. We smile. My son notices the black stains of fires still present, or is it the dampness of the rock inside showing itself in streaks? We all notice the closeness of one family to another. The closeness of people to river. The way life must have gathered on the banks of the river in a unified respect and need. We all feel the presence and the power of time. Of life. Of ceremony.

The main attraction at this site are the rock paintings. White paint on red rock. Stick figures speaking through symbolism. And one of them, spoken about in many prophecies and teachings, is of a stair case. The painting shows the line of life, a human, a stair case, a choice, and two potential outcomes. One side of the stair case leads up and up, over a plateau and into the sky. The other continues on its same flat motion and comes to an earlier stopping point. Information encoded in this painting may be unlocked at length through contemplation.

For the purposes of this writing let us look at just the surface, or obvious message this prophetic painting conveys[3]. Human is walking on Earth, or with the Earth, along the road of time, through deep antiquity to the present. At the present juncture, a staircase emerges. Human may either step up, ascending in rapid, spiralling arcs, into a new level of consciousness – or – he/she may continue walking with the same eyes that have served him/her until now. Like a cooking pot that has been well used, but whose bottom is thinning, our present perception will no longer serve the purpose of our existence.

The steps we are facing now are fully exposed in front of us. If we have courage, we might use a viral pandemic to wake ourselves up to other concerns we have covered over. Utilising our ability to gather, to organise and share a common cause, we might demand the disarmament of nuclear weapons globally before we cooperate with any further legislation regarding a pandemic[4]. We might insist on seed banks in every locality, and the right to gather on land for the purposes of growing our own food. We might draw the line at extinction ourselves. For we do have a responsibility to the generations coming ahead of us. It is simply not our prerogative to allow their possibility for life to dissolve.

Consent

From different sectors and different locations, thought leaders have spoken of militarised lockdowns in relation to our right to reason, or to receive and make sense of information on our own (Gupta, 2021; Eisenstein, 2020). Militarised lockdowns have happened many times before. And incomplete disclosure of government intention has also happened. It is a possibility that it is happening now.

In 1992 a global summit met in Rio de Janeiro with the intention to create a plan to address climate change and trade. The summit was made up of economic as well as political leaders. Issues relating to population, the movement of goods and resources and national securities were on the table. What came out of that meeting is known as Agenda 21 and the contents of that agenda are publicly available (United Nations, 1992). Within the lengthy document

---

3 For an absolutely beautiful and deep message about this glyph, please see Masayesva (2020).

4 There are also prophecies within the indigenous tribes of the Americas that speak to a possible moment of nuclear fallout. They describe a sky turning red and water which looks clean but which kills. They counsel that those who may survive will live far from others, underneath blankets of deep snow.

are many good and reasonable ideas. However, the direction the agenda sets on course leads ultimately to further and further restrictions on freedom of movement. These include the movement of people into dense, urban living conditions where social monitoring is constant. Our ability to leave the urban environments would be heavily curtailed. Our ability to trade outside of established currencies would be limited. And our freedom of choice over healthcare would be determined by governing and expert bodies. This would all be in the interests of protecting nature.

In 2019 a computer simulation known as Event 201 was created to show the flow of potential responses to a possible pandemic. Recommendations following on from the exercise include protection for global and international businesses, protection for global and international trade, the securing of resources for the mass production of vaccines and efforts to censor and curb misinformation (Event 201, 2019). The Johns Hopkins Centre for Health Security ran two previous exercises, one for a smallpox outbreak and one for a bioterrorism attack. Such exercises are not in and of themselves alarming. Within context, however, it is worth taking note of.

It is a cool day in the autumn of 2017. The university where I lecture has recently been through complete overhaul of its leadership and management. There are new people, new ideas and new funding protocols. I am going to a meeting on the new agendas, so that I might effectively obtain support for a project I am keen to start. As I sit down to the meeting the first thing I notice is that I am the only person from the arts. I chat with the lecturer next to me, who is hoping to get support for his project in business studies. As the presentation begins I get out my pen and paper to jot down notes. Within the first few minutes however, I pause. By the end of the meeting, I have made up my mind to leave the university within the year. (2017)

What was shared at that meeting floored me. Years later, as the presented scenarios began to unfold, I wish I had taken photos. For me, they came as no surprise. For what we were told is that under the European Research Council and the World Health Organization, our university had agreed to only support bids in line with new sustainability initiatives: the objectives of which were to create vaccines and to develop 5G technology. We were told that 6 billion vaccines were going to be needed by 2021. We were told that 5G technology would go in first in London, Detroit, Los Angeles, Wuhan, Milan and

Moscow. After that it would spread to smaller cities and then to every location worldwide. The technology would be utilised to track the movement of every member of society, down to the facial muscles. Further, cash would be slowly eliminated. Billions of euros/pounds/dollars were available for anyone wanting to contribute to the research[5].

The ideas presented here are not new. Disclosure, while public, may remain largely out of the public mind or knowledge. And the tilting of information toward agendas other than the true health of the people is not new. Throughout civilisation, we humans have chosen to enslave, withhold and disempower. Many generations of people have lived through terrible totalitarian regimes. Many generations of people have endured torture and confinement.

Care

As I witness the human in all of her beauty, it is how we care for each other that touches me most deeply. This is indeed what has carried us through. So strong is our sense of care that we willingly give our lives for another. We will give our food, clothes and resources to a person, child or animal in need. And we give our time, our presence, our ears and our very heart power to each other. And so it is, with the most powerful of our gifts, that they are sometimes co-opted for agendas other than their own pure expression.

One of the ways care is co-opted is through the connection of it to ideals. With an ideal of saving the world from ethnic genocide, a world war was justified. With an ideal of ensuring freedom from slavery, the American Civil War was justified. With an ideal of saving a people from the undemocratic forces of their own government, a Cold War, a Korean War, a Vietnam War and many other wars in many other places were justified. The care we as humans have for each other and by which we will sacrifice our own wellbeing, our own self-preservation, our very lives has been called on as permission for warfare. The reality is that many of these wars were not in fact about ideals or freedom. They were about resources, and the channelling of resources from one area of the world to another. Reaping the spoils of these resources, we in the 'Western' world all too easily allowed our sense of care to be co-opted. We did not ask the fuller questions. Questions such as 'Must so many die in order to change this

---

5 Additionally, it was explained to us that standard human rights procedures for research would not be necessary. They were too time-consuming in the face of impending climate crisis. And smart technology was needed urgently to address the crisis. The specific agendas my university was supporting would exist within the ERC alongside research into other measures of sustainability.

situation?', 'Are there other possible alternatives?', 'What choices would bring about peace for all involved here?'.

Many of us have family and loved ones who have died in war. And they have been brave. And much courage has been shown from human to human. The linking of duty and care are what the machinations of profit have steadily appealed to. Our potent human capacity for care has been appropriated by the 'sovereigns' of our nations for purposes of monetary gain and resources.

And those who would serve such machinations, knowingly or in ignorance, have become expert at tuning our emotional fields. When emotion becomes strong, and ungrounded from the heart, we become capable of horrible things, believing we are acting from a bigger source. And we are. But that source is not the indwelling of universal love made manifest through the heart. Emotions are easily manipulated. And so the impulse of the human to look after and care for each other becomes tied to fear, loss, grief and anger.

Our care for each other and the Earth is infinitely huge and natural and good. Our sense of connection is important. And it is a wonderful impulse to follow. When we feel connected we feel free within ourselves, and share freely. The key is to tune ourselves to the perceptual frequencies of love and the Earth herself. Taking full responsibility for the stories we live and the emotions we cultivate, we begin to place ourselves back in the place of our own power. Together, we are generative, creative. We are empowered. For we recognise that our power arises from the love within us. True love seeks the benefit for all. Love will not harm, nor will it suffer needlessly. Love will not send its children or its elderly away to die, and love will not imprison itself. In the realms of power and consent, sovereignty and love are inextricably linked.

There are many possibilities for what is actually happening. From a higher perspective, all of it is occurring because we are thinking, feeling and imagining it. All possibilities exist within our collective mind. And if we desire to shift ourselves out of scenarios that are alienating or harmful, then we might begin to focus our minds on that which we do want to create. There is a balance between seeing clearly and acting with care. Some would call that a balance between reason and emotion. Others would pair the mind with the heart. As different veils lift off our eyes, each one of us in our own timing and way, we will feel many things. Those feelings are indicators to us. We don't want to feed feelings that take us out of balance and health. We can, however, trust the wisdom of our deeper selves when it speaks.

Like reciprocity and nature, power and consent are foundational and symbiotic concepts – without each other they do not stand. When we give away power, we also give away our right, or ability, to consent. The goodness of our human nature may then be easily co-opted.

Money

Another way we allow the co-opting of our power is through our engagement with money. Money is energy. Money is exchange. And while money itself is not a bad thing, as a way to exchange energy for the benefit of all, our underlying tendencies toward greed and entitlement can distort our good intentions. Issues arise when humans divorce any part of our structures from kindness and care. And that applies to nature, physical health, assertion of power and the exchange of money equally.

Alanis Obomsawin, an Abenaki from the Odanak tribe of North America, is attributed as saying, 'When the last tree is cut, the last fish is caught, and the last river is polluted; when to breathe the air is sickening, you will realise, too late, that wealth is not in bank accounts and that you can't eat money' (Obomsawin, no date). This statement, whether spoken by Obomsawin or another, rings true. At this moment in time we are in the late-stage throes of monopoly capitalism. While some argue that capitalism itself will fix the problem, through a need to profit from solutions, I personally feel that the underlying issues of the human condition are too strongly imprinted in the current model for it to effectively refocus itself. Many thinkers have focused on the renewal of earlier barter systems – rooted at a local level – as plausible working solutions. I feel, however, that we are on the brink of new vantage points that would create prosperity and abundance for all. The barter system may work within small groups who are self-organised around care. As we globally address our needs across nations and peoples, however, we cannot now extricate ourselves from the compounding issues of climate crisis and the detritus of globalism. A combination of local solutions and universal human values is our true hope. As exemplified by Obomsawin, wealth itself is the concept that requires redress. Indigenous peoples the world over perceive wealth not as accumulation, but by the ability to have enough to share. If we tend to our intrinsic sense of care and turn it towards a sense of global unity, might we create solutions that are not dependent on large-scale policy? This is both an interior and an exterior consideration. For humans to place true abundance, physical as well as spiritual, at the core of exchange, we are required to look deeply into our own position within the collective mind.

According to Sufi scholars of the 20th century, specifically those stemming from the perennialist school of thought (Guenon, 2009) the global situation we see at the moment is simply the outcome of seeds sown in our consciousness long ago. Seeds, when planted, grow forests. The solutions we desire may not come from digging up our old forests, but from the planting of new seeds. I value this perspective as it encourages us to plant new seeds which have in their imprint something that can be grown between us, for the unity of coming generations. Slowly, the old will fall away. It already is. And as we naturally begin to create new lifestyles, our local necessities and the impulses of our developing evolutionary states may converge in exciting possibilities which only a year or two ago we could not imagine.

From an economic perspective, both world wars and the current pandemic have resulted in the movement of profits from local sources toward larger, national and corporate entities. From a perspective of sovereignty, it is following the Second World War that dependence on corporate farming and global issues of food scarcity came into being. And it is in the wake of a global pandemic that issues of personal sovereignty regarding our bodies and freedoms of movement are being taken. If we look further back however, these wars and pandemics are more like surface boils, the visible symptoms of thought that was cultivated much earlier.

From a spiritual perspective, the oppositional movement or antidote has been steadily and patiently cultivated as well. From the indigenous elders who carried values of reciprocity and care through time, to the spiritual teachers who have emerged in each age, we have had reminders to turn ourselves towards our true capacities for love. Each of the masters, from Buddha to Jesus to the many unnamed women and men who have carried the flame of the heart, have encouraged us to love each other, take care of each other, to let go of a need for accumulation and to see the full love of the universe within each and every one. It is up to us to recognise that machinations of profit have grown deep roots within our collective psyche, entwining themselves with the power of all that is good within us. To free ourselves from these same machinations, we might begin with cultivating the freedom of our own hearts. Are we in a right relationship with money, power and care? Such interior steps are not so small, they are the task of the moment, for we are forming a collective blueprint that we will pass on to the coming generations.

Level Three: Energy for Change
The third level is centred at the solar plexus. It is located between the curves of the ribs, along the mid thoracic spine. At this centre willpower and action are our main concerns. The emotions of joy and anger vacillate here, presenting us

with an ever-constant choice about where we act from. The colour of the third centre is yellow and the associated element is fire. While survival and emotion govern the first two major centres of the spine, it is the fire of desire that turns the wheel of the third. At this level we may build a bridge between the three lower centres and the heart.

A bridge is a metaphor as well as a functional tool. In the third centre we look at population levels, technology, and potential innovation, which may assist us in moving collectively toward the heart. How we make use of that which we create, how we relate to it, what limitations we give it and the directions we choose to advance it in are of great consequence. For we have choices before us, in terms of embracing artificial intelligence, robots and electricity-dependent resources. From an astrological stance, we are moving now into the age of Aquarius. Aquarian ages are known for their radical innovation and use of technologies. But because we are continually in a new position within our larger galaxy, each major age or cycle does not resemble the one before. We are at juncture not dissimilar in scale to our shift from hunter-gatherer peoples to peoples who built and lived in cities. As we move out of the age of cities and settled civilisations, we might seriously imagine whole new ways of approaching habitat and design. The technologies we have today may seem crudely outdated in the not-too-distant future.

Population

Take kindly the council of the earth,
Gracefully surrounding the things of youth.
Nurture the strength of spirit to shield you in sudden misfortunes,
But do not distress yourself with imaginings.
Many fears are born in fatigue and loneliness,
Beyond the wholesome discipline. Be gentle with yourself.
You are a child of the universe, no less than the trees and stars.
You have a right to be here. And whether or not it is clear to you,
No doubt the universe is unfolding as it should.
Be at peace with God, whatever you conceive him/her to be.
And whatever your labours, and aspirations,
In the noisy confusion of life, keep peace with your soul.
With all the sham, drudgery and broken dreams,
It is still a beautiful world. Be cheerful, and strive to be happy.
Elders of the Lakota Nation (2019)

Planet Earth loves to birth, to watch us grow, to celebrate our travails and our choices, to celebrate our beauty and our flowering. Life is a part of Earth.

And we are the stewards of life. For every one of us was born of a womb – male or female, if we birth children or we don't, however we identify. And the pain of our mothers is real within our bones, our blood. Every one of them sacrificed her time, her love and her very body for you to exist at all. With freedom, you have moved into your own path, your own life. And yet still, the mother will always hold you. For as much as the wombs of this Earth have carried in pain, there is beauty.

What if the number of people currently on Earth is not an accident, but facilitation by the Earth herself to move her people into a different level of consciousness? It may be that the Earth actually requires the power of the human heart x billions in order to facilitate her own leap of consciousness. For the Earth is the mother of the mothers. It is by her kindness that we are here. And it may take all nine billion of us to create a light strong enough to burn away the shadow she has carried. Rather than drown, freeze or incinerate us, she – and we – may be ready to come together with awareness and reverence for our singular shared heart.

Overpopulation is a myth. I may receive critique for positioning myself thus; however, it is my inner conviction. The Earth can support all of her people, and all those that will come after, and is happy to do so. When we are in balance, she is in balance. Our issues have to do with the giving over of reproductive choice directly to the women who carry life, as well as wealth inequality and overconsumption. These issues often dovetail, with the least well-off having the least choice over their reproductive cycles. If we are to address climate change from humanitarian perspectives we must necessarily move our focus away from overpopulation and toward distribution and lifestyle.

When we bring women to the forefront of conversation and debate, we bring the value of life to the table. Women produce life. And life has value, it is a precious gift. If we are billions, then our means of stewardship must shift. To accommodate each other, among our animal and plant relations, we likely need to move away from single-family households. We likely need to let go of an overabundance of personal goods. We will have to shift away from foods that take more resources to produce than the life they give in digestion. What will it mean to live vegetarian or vegan, to live within community and to live simply? A mother does not take the lives of some of her children so that her others might have larger bedrooms and fancy cars. A mother becomes more resourceful. She moves house, facilitates deeper care, goes without food herself if need be.

Together, we can do it. We are incredible at problem solving when we put our hearts together. What foods must we cultivate, what methods of farming? What governing structures support the local and the communal? How do we support each other through the emotions and attachments that do not allow us to embrace wholeheartedly the changes we must make?

Interdependence

Interdependence can be defined as the symbiotic interrelationship of parts to a whole. Connected to reciprocity and care, interdependence becomes a grounded idea as it translates to permaculture and regeneration. The whole is complete as each part is fully lived and thriving.

Interdependence depends on individuals who choose to live fully in love. As avenues of care open between us, cooperation then ceases to be an ideal. Cooperation becomes an embodied state of grace by which inner and outer harmonise. Cooperation becomes a state of mercy whereby the eyes of the heart behold all that is seen as love.

Dependence can be defined as the inverse of interdependence. Parts are replaceable. Diversity is homogenised. Beauty, texture and harmony have less value. Reproduction can be done *en masse*. And without warmth. Dependence puts systems in place to provide everything from goods to leadership to basic parenting. And from a space of dependence, humans may even become reliant on systems to provide answers for how we think and how we feel[6]. We have lived in a state of dependency for quite some time in the developed world. And for all our resources and material wealth, we are mentally and emotionally unstable and unhappy, for the large part. Dependence is just not going to work for us much longer.

As humans, we are creators. And where we create from is vital to the form and quality of what is created. It is our belief in what we imagine that brings it into form. We believe in money. And we believe in authority. We believe in scarcity. And we believe in differences of value.

Belief is powerful as it is the harness by which the mind moves ideas into action. People will die for belief, they will move across the world for belief, they will have children and marry for belief, and they will go to war and kill for what they believe in. If we can pause for a moment to consider belief as

---

6 Dependence on God is another matter altogether. To shift a settled perspective of dependence, it can be useful to move our sense of reliance to the divine. For it is by the divine that we have breath and life in the first instance. Across spiritual and indigenous traditions, it is the movement of divine desire by which existence is.

something not fixed, not solid, we can see the power of imagination to shift underlying beliefs. When we can imagine something different, whole new avenues open up for creation.

It is my faith in the human heart that sees a future unfolding where issues of resources and exchange are handled first and foremost from a vantage point of care. Where creativity and creation are valued. In the future I see, each person is witnessed as a universe unto themselves. Surrounded by beautiful reflections of each other, our meeting points become spaces of fruitful imaginings. As humans in their full creative power, care is the currency by which we choose to exchange. We choose. Because we have each chosen to live fully inside of love, the spaces of our meeting become a touchstone for the flowering of health and abundance.

Energy

Transition town is a movement that was started in 2006 in Devon, England. It sought to reduce the effects of peak oil, climate change and transition. By bringing communities together to plant and grow food, share cars and support each other in a mixture of small but important ways, resilience was built. The idea spread and over 2,000 transition towns were recognised within the network (Rapid Transition Alliance, 2019). I myself lived for a few years in a neighbourhood that identified as part of the movement.

Plenty is a currency originating in the Ithaca area of upstate New York. The model is based on an exchange of hours, whereby one hour is worth a certain amount of plenty. Plenty can be used at local shops, grocers, service providers and even to pay your rent. The model was so catching that it was instated elsewhere. For example, the Chapel Hill area of North Carolina created the NCPlenty.

Examples such as this illustrate energy in motion. The jumps we have to make may not in fact be that difficult, or without precedence. And we can go further. Many people speak of Nikola Tesla and his dream that electricity could be freely resourced from the air, at every home, with zero impact on the environment and zero exchange of currencies[7].

The third centre is where energy is mobilised and focused. On our way to a beautiful, rejuvenating, zero impact way of life, we may see innovations arise and fall away again rather rapidly. This is all right. For the innovations or

---

7 Nikola Tesla (1856–1943) is credited with the design of the the alternating current supply system, as well as radar, X-rays and hydroelectric generation. Tesla's Free Energy Project was a dream that was not realised before his death.

inventions that are best suited to each people and each location are the ones which will be adopted and refined for future generations. Once again, how we utilise the energy we create is as important as what we create. Does everyone benefit? Is anyone harmed?

Arthur Firstenburg is a researcher who wrote of the symptoms and causes of electricity poisoning early in our societal adoption of it. Pulling together studies which detail the early effects of travel by train, the installation of lights and wires to households and other rudimentary electrical uses within society, Firstenburg shows that the potential dangers of electricity exposure were known early on. Excitement about what electricity could offer caught our imaginations, however, and this paved the way to our current dependence and overuse (2020).

Electricity is natural, existing both in the environment and our bodies. Cellular communication depends on micro-vibrations of the piezoelectric frequencies[8]. Electricity poisoning can occur, however, and is most dramatically demonstrated in the use of the electric chair. Through the onset of smart cities, smart cars and smart homes – all powered by 5G – we may enter a period of increased electrical usage. Symptoms of electricity poisoning include:

- Shortness of breath
- Muscle cramps
- Seizure
- Paralysis
- Respiratory failure
- Overheating
- Neurological meltdown

Initial responses may also include headaches, fatigue, foggy brain and finally a release of mucus. If electricity poisoning gets to the point where the lungs fill with fluid, it is due to rapid cell die-off and the subsequent waste produced.

I mention these symptoms to bring awareness of the potential effects of electricity on our systems should we choose to continue increasing the electrical field of our homes and lives. What level of crude electrical exposure is actually

---

8 The piezoelectric communication of cells has been known to energy healers such as Dr Randolph Stone (1986a; 1986b), and the ancient Vedic for a very long time. Its use within crystal technologies has been employed throughout the 20th century. Applications of these currents in cellular signalling have been a topic of Western scientific research since about 2005.

safe for the human system? What are alternatives that both excite and inspire us? And are we ready to follow the example of small villages across Africa and Asia, which have begun to generate and distribute their own electricity, independent of any company or corporation? What happens when we begin to create our own economic and energy sovereignty?

Nature

Nature is a vast and living organism. Every part of her functions in relation to her whole. Symbiosis is her natural state. Extensive networks of communication move across her every fibre. In our connection to her we dissolve into the greater expanse of our being. She is intelligent. And if we extend the boundaries of her body, we might find ways of living within and surrounded by her once again. Ways that echo ancient principles and universal law, yet look radically different. For example, sensitive, responsive homes made of living mycelium may soon be possible (Davies, 2021). And frontiers are opening in the areas of design and habitat through creative application of music and sound. We can think bigger and we can dream brighter. For while online portals may relieve the pressures of both loneliness and income generation, they may distract us from developing true ingenuity. As our interaction with technology continues to increase, what will help us most is a further increase in our interaction with nature.

Can a symbiosis of technology and nature be hoped for? Does a human body share in that symbiosis with ease and graceful stewardship? Putting aside notions of the cyborg, we might imagine surprising and new relationships to our technologies. Relationships which place sentience, connection and love at the centre. Nature is not artificial. And it may be that one day we look back on the internet itself as a crude representation of our own awakened and interconnected telepathic abilities. As we are able to reduce dependence on electricity and crude mechanisms, what might we discover? Could new understandings of technologies, as forces of both power and nature, emerge through sound and vibration?

The psycho-spiritual-body is alive across its manifest levels. What is good for one part must be good for the whole. As the third centre is the seat of willpower, transformation and joy – we may look to our natural wellsprings of joy to guide us in our questioning and endeavours. There is no right and there is no wrong in the solutions we create. We have only to try and try again, refining the heart and deepening her connection each time. Evolution is a process, and we are active agents within it.

Chapter Two
Seven Levels: Levels Four to Seven

Level Four: A Bridge

Each one of us has known, either dimly inside or with great clarity, that the way of life we have created over the last few thousand years is not sustainable. We have enjoyed the plush gratifications of easy shelter, easy food and a sense of being all important – at least in the West and the 'developed' world. And we have known, we have known deep inside, that our ease has come at a huge cost to others. Others who live in deplorable conditions, mothers who cannot feed their children, children who work 12–15–18 hours a day for our self-justified gratifications. And we have rallied, protested, proclaimed on behalf of equality. But equality has never really come. For even as rights have been 'given' to children, to women, and finally to nature, those rights have not fully translated into health and freedom for the weakest of society. Rights that are inherent to existence and life need not be 'given'.

And so, God in all of his/her mercy has allowed us to create an unreal situation, an impossible checkmate. And here we are, with governments we do not believe in issuing us morsels of rights we no longer have a full and legal claim to. We are told where and when we may travel, whom we may speak with and see, what we may speak, and what hours of the day we are allowed outside. Many countries the world over have lived under such conditions for decades at a time or longer. This is the first time that such control has been wielded on a global scale, however, and this is significant. The outer world is a reflection of the inner. The prisons we are living in are not all of brick and mortar. They are the structures that we feed within our minds. It is time that we see more clearly. It is time we elevate ourselves to see with the eyes of the heart.

How many of us are truly aware of our heart? Just as we have separated ourselves from our bodies, we have also allowed our hearts to atrophy. We have forgotten the beauty of a fresh dawn. We no longer hear the voices of the waterfalls and the stars. The eyes of the heart see in ways that the mind is not able to categorise, explain or put into linear place.

The fourth centre is the centre of the heart – both the physical, beating heart and the metaphysical one. The heart forms a bridge between the lower centres, which are focused on our base energies and will power, to our true desire. As the fire of the third centre rises the heart begins to warm. In Sufism, the human heart is considered to be the jewel of all the universes. We are the only beings created with free will, and as we learn to direct the energies of the heart we literally create reality. So the consideration with which we approach the heart forms the way we live on Earth, and perhaps beyond. The frequencies we emit from the heart centre, electromagnetic in their physical form, bring matter into manifestation. At the fourth level we have the opportunity to purify the energies of the lower centres so that we direct our creative capacities toward beauty. And this life is beautiful. We have the opportunity to create heaven on earth, and it is the dreaming of the heart that brings beauty into form upon the planet. If our desire is to pass a world of abundance, health and kindness to the coming generations we must necessarily engage the heart in the process.

There is a vast potential in the heart that we have yet to realise collectively. In this chapter I bring in the perspectives of various spiritual traditions to highlight the depth of possibility we have right now.

The Way of the Kahuna

The way of the heart is a way of self-responsibility. Such a stance insists on sovereignty as its foundation. For when trusting the heart we must be prepared to accept and act upon what the heart reveals. The heart is the seat of love, and our understanding of love, like most things, matures as we mature. A young love is full of wonder, a developing love will encounter pain, and a love that is maturing engages stages of self-awareness, which ultimately lead to a love filled with inspiration, power and grace. A maturing love is powerful and kind, and approaches the kind of spiritual love we might call unconditional, for it refuses to blame, shame or harm any other. And so responsibility becomes a touchstone of that love, a foundational aspect to the heart. For once we begin to live from love and surrender ever more deeply to it, that life might not look like we thought it would!

In Hawaiian shamanism the big shamans, the elders of the path, are called kahunas. They carry teachings on love that we in the contemporary West might find radical. These teachings are useful, as we negotiate change, and so I introduce them here.

Joe Vitale is an elder, a kahuna, of the Hawaiian tradition. He speaks of the ho'oponopono teachings they practice as a space of zero limits (2009). Vitale, like many spiritual masters, has often carried on a regular life, working a regular job while also teaching and seeing people in a flow of reciprocity. At a certain point, he found himself working as a night guard at a large mental institution. As he engaged the energies of the place, he began to apply the principles of ho'oponopono to the situation, and radical change ensued. The principles of ho'oponopono state that we as individuals are responsible for everything that appears in our lives. If we are witnessing or on the receiving end of any form of disjuncture, then those same qualities come back to and stem from a deep source within us. In order to shift the qualities and realities that we perceive in our daily lives, we must stand in a place of complete acceptance and self-responsibility for them. And so, from this place of acceptance, we begin to pray. The ho'oponopono prayer is simple yet powerful. It states,

Please forgive me, for any harm I have caused to you, in this or any other lifetime.

I forgive you for any harm that you have caused to me, in this or any other lifetime.

Thank you for being here, for forgiving me. Thank you for receiving my forgiveness.

I love you and I am sorry.

Within a year of using this prayer with each and every one of the inmates at the mental institution, every one of them had been freed. The institution was empty, and Vitale had to find another job!

I work with this prayer regularly, and guide many of my students and clients through it. As you read this, if you are touched, you might choose to sit and engage this prayer now:

Forgiveness exercise
1. Create a clean space, light a candle and burn some sweet-smelling incense or herbs. Turn off any distractions, close the doors, and centre yourself in the place of your heart. Sit yourself down and wait until you become still.
2. Now imagine the person you would like to forgive. Imagine them as you last remember them, and invite them to sit in front of you.
3. As the person arrives, notice them fully. What are they wearing, what are their mannerisms, what colours surround them?

4. When the person is settled say to them 'Thank you for being here. I really appreciate your coming. I would like to ask you to forgive me, for any harm I have caused to you, in this or any other lifetime'.
5. Wait as the person receives your request. Observe them as they begin to offer you forgiveness. What changes in their mannerisms, and how do the colours around them change? Become aware of a golden thread moving between yourself and the other, and watch how it is cleansing, brightening. Receive their forgiveness with gratitude and love.
6. Then, when you are ready say to them, 'I also forgive you, for any harm you have done to me, in this or any other lifetime'.
7. Wait as the person receives your forgiveness. As they do, observe yourself. What changes in your mannerisms, and how do the colours around you change? Watch as they receive your forgiveness fully. Allow gratitude and love to flow freely between you.
8. When you are ready, you may say to them, 'Thank you for being here. I truly appreciate this opportunity to be in forgiveness with you. You may depart now'.
9. Watch with loving attention as they go. Be aware of their mannerisms, their colours, as they leave the moment you have shared. Say to yourself, 'I love you and I am sorry'. Receive this.
10. As you return to yourself, feel the weight and reality of your own body, become aware of the space you are sitting in, and centre yourself once again in your own heart.

The transition space of the fourth centre requires only that we open our perception to it, with sincerity and humbleness. For the heart of love is more vast than we can possibly comprehend. We are at this time of change releasing all that does not serve: the stories, the shame, the guilt, the pain, the dirt, the weakness, the complicity in wounding and in suffering, the victim and the perpetrator. All of it now goes. God, love, Allah has gifted us this time to let go of all that we have engaged and created, so that heaven on earth may be manifest. And heaven is a place where love manifests as beauty, because we stand in the sovereign place of the heart and choose it.

Thank you this morning Allah, Great Spirit, love, for the opportunity to release more fully. Thank you for the opportunity to accept my fellow human beings as they are, and to choose love. May I keep letting go as I continue to open. (2021)

The Great Wound

At this moment in time we have been given a great gift, the gift of time. For within time things are slowed down. We have the opportunity to offer an intervention. So in our space of transition, we are able to come to the place where we value each other, we value life, and we value our sacred contract with life. We come to a space where we can learn to use time and our energies wisely. And as part of this we will face mortality and death. In the first chakra centre, death is a physical reality to face. In the fourth centre, as it rises to meet to the heart, death becomes one of the ways we value life.

For me, to face mortality and death begins with looking closely at my relationship with my mother. It has never been great. She has tried her best; however, she has endured much, and life has not given her as much wonder as it has difficulty. In the wake of globally restricted movement, I had to face the idea that she may become ill and pass, and I may not get to see her. To live my days without resolving the great wound would not be acceptable to me. To let her potentially pass without grace, love and forgiveness would cause a great rift in my soul. So I had to reassess who I am and my relationship to her. Because if I carry and pass on great teachings from spiritual traditions, then I myself must live them.

The great wound is the wound of separation. On a spiritual level, it is separation from unity with God, with love, which causes us suffering and pain. On a physical level, it is separation from the mother which is the counterpoint. The mother wound and the wound of separation are one and the same thing. As we enter the earth, we are one with our mother in her body. The process of birth is traumatic because we physically become separate from her. We gasp, we cry. We need nourishment from respiration to begin to live as our own body. Then sometime before the second birthday, we begin to separate again, on a more emotional level. Realising that we have our own will and desires, we begin the painful process by declaring 'No!'. The young child discovers then that their body, with a boundary of skin, has a will and a mind that is its own.

During these early years, the reality of our separate existence comes as quite a shock. Having grown inside the womb, with a deep connection to mother as the very source of life, the challenge to step out on our own may produce deep insecurity. In an ideal situation, where the bond with the mother is healthy and strong, she is able to encourage and facilitate our emerging sense of separate self. The young child may move into the world full of curiosity and confidence. But if the heart connection is not strong between the mother and child, for any reason we might imagine, the child may become fearful. If the mother was separated from the child for instance, if she dealt with abuse, mental strain or hormonal imbalance, or if the mother simply lacks awareness and support to encourage her child's independence, the child will face the wound of separation alone. The assertion of their will may become challenging for them, and they may act out of insecurity or become problematic. Even for those who are held with love, however, the realisation of our separation is a very big deal. As we boil this down, however, the truth is that we are never fully alone. The innocent, the young, are protected on the deepest spiritual levels. And when we have to face the great wound alone, it merely provides an early impulse to seek God and love as the resource for addressing this wound.

The separation from the mother is known in spiritual traditions as the great wound because it mirrors the wound of our separation from unity, from the source of love from which we came. As we enter this earthly plane, we are formed in bodies of flesh which are bounded in time and space. With these bodies come wonderful opportunities for joy and life. And as part of our earthly journey, we must walk with these bodies as beings of our own free will, separate from the unified state of pre-creation.

As I work with the energies of the great wound myself, I look to both my earthly mother and to the body of earth from which my bones are made. I am comprised of soil, water and air. My breath comes from the wind of this planet and I am intrinsically connected to the body of the Earth herself. In this reciprocity, this knowing, the greater wound is softened. I am able to experience and know that I belong here. My life has value here. And by the engagement of my free will, I can create beauty for myself and others. I can create beauty with the body of earth from which I spring.

Resting in the embrace of the Earth, I am able to be present with the fleshly body that birthed me, the heart and soul of my ancestral mother, with due respect and kindness. In my understanding so far, separation is necessary in order to activate and form our free will. Whether that happens with joy and protection, or without, is of less consequence than I might care to recognise. In the bigger picture of lives, I may rest with the flesh and bones of my earthly mother in gratitude for this opportunity for life. Moving on from a place of insecurity or fear, I may now action my free will towards choosing love. And to choose to love the mothers that birthed us is perhaps the first and most important act of forgiveness and self-responsibility the heart desires.

Facing Fear and Trauma

The primal brain is located in the cerebellum, or the brain stem which moves from the base of the brain into the spinal column. The brain stem is like a highway for information from the nervous system, moving information from the perimeter of the body – skin, eyes, etc. – to the core. Within the brain stem are stored the collective memories of the species. The cerebellum is a necessary part of our evolutionary system because it is useful for survival. As information moves up the spinal column and through the brain stem it passes through the stored, collective memory. Our responses are weighted accordingly, and in times when a perceived threat to survival is recognised, the brain will give a signal of fight, flight or freeze to the body. These responses are known as trauma; however, they are completely natural, and protective.

Moving beyond the primal brain and its fear responses is a crucial step on the path to both personal and collective healing. Through the circumstance of a global pandemic, we are as a species beginning to recognise the power of our environment and relationships to our health. Moving through the trauma we have together lived and witnessed is an important part of boiling and releasing the energies of the lower centres, which is necessary to walk over the bridge to our heart. In the past few centuries especially, we have participated in ungodly amounts of warfare, slavery, imprisonment and harm. And it is notable that we, as a collective, are responding to a moment of pandemic as if it too were a war to fight, a war that could be won. The body is not a chamber for war. To view it as thus causes it to freeze, dissociate or die. The body is a holy temple, that longs and needs to walk freely among nature, to touch and to be touched, to eat of the fruits and plants of the earth in order to heal. As we imprison ourselves, in order to save ourselves, we are avoiding facing our fear of death. We are avoiding facing the trauma deeply present in our bodies and our histories. We are forgetting that it is only in facing our traumas and our fears that we might create solutions that both heal us and respect our inherent needs.

Shaman Alberto Villolodo writes that releasing fear is a necessary stage that we progress through in order to experience freedom from illusion. As our internal projections and illusions fade into a distant past, where they belong, energy is made available with which to dream a new world into being (2010). And it is this ability to dream a new world into being that is uniquely human, for it rests upon the heart. What we are able to imagine, we create. If we continue to imagine death, separation, contagion, control and violence, then we will have more of it. But if we support each other to vivify our imaginations toward the continuation of life, then we will have it. For we are in this togeth-

41

er, and we will pass through this together. And together, we will move through the waters of our emotions. For as we encounter our fears and release them, emotion will certainly arise.

Emotion is both biological and psychological. Because of the way emotion is rooted in the limbic system, it is almost always tied to the past. When we are young, our understanding of reality is based on feedback we get from the world. As we respond we receive further feedback, and this creates a neurological groove or loop. As a child our needs for vulnerability, belonging, security and love are established. In our early years, the way these needs are met or unmet forms the foundation of our individual response to the world – and our sense of reality.

Because we have lived through several centuries where belonging, vulnerability and safety have not been largely available, healthy adaptation is not something we as a 'Western' or globalised collective generally embody. For example, we know as a species that we have polluted the earth to the point of collapse, yet we are only beginning to adapt in significant ways. As our global responses to pandemic, climate and psychological changes continue to transform and evolve, and as emotion rises, another thing that's going to come up for people is a questioning of reality. When our doors of perception begin to open, it can be greatly unsettling. That unsettling will take us right back to the early years of our lives and the original wound. And with that, we will each face our need to belong, to be vulnerable, to have clear information and to be safe.

The old, outdated, primal responses we are bringing to bear on our current crises will only serve to reinforce the fight, flight, freeze paradigms held in our bodies. We do, however, have the time and opportunity right now to change track. Moving through these layers together, we have a chance to release our collective cellular programming. As we do so, we create space in our collective psyche to form new structures. And these structures are best forged in the chambers of the heart.

I myself have cried on many days. I've cried at the horror of what's going on. I've cried in anger. I've cried in helplessness, and in loneliness. Having an opportunity to look at these emotions and the space to let them move through has been important. Connecting to our Mother Earth, touching earth, allowing her to hold me has also been important. And having others to connect to. So when I talk about our emotions and our necessity for each other, I speak from that place of universality and change. If we can go to the place at the centre of the heart, we find a great light. And the strength of that light offers us the resilience to move through the traumas, the wounds and the waters of our emotions.

The attributes of the heart are forgiveness and compassion. As reciprocity and care rise through the fire of the third centre into the fourth, they ignite inspiration and compassion on a spiritual level. As you look at the journey you have travelled, you might extend to yourself a loving compassionate appreciation. For we have each carried so much. And in acceptance of all that we have carried, the burden may soften and enter the fire of transformation. Acceptance, without judgement, leads to the dissolution of fear. For when we accept a thing we put ourselves into a relationship of agency with that same thing. Here the realms of dependency and sovereignty are transmuted – and we come to accept that all of life, down to our very breath, is a gift from love. Wrought in the fire of surrender to a greater love, the new – or true – human beings begin to emerge.

Level Five: Emergence
The fifth level has everything to do with the throat, the voice, with structure and freedom and togetherness. It is a place of emergence and will be the central focus of the next era. For we as humanity are emerging from one world to the next.

There are many perspectives and cosmologies I could draw from to speak to this level and this moment of emergence. All of them have some truth and are valuable as guide maps. Similar to the concept of seven levels, where you are looking from determines what you will see. In this section I introduce the emergence stories of the North American indigenous peoples. Drawing mostly from Navajo cosmologies, I tell the story of how we emerged from the first world to the second, the second to the third and the third to the fourth. These worlds speak to the major phases of human evolution on our planet – and as such the worlds look vastly different in each phase. Some are filled with water, others with light. At one moment we shifted into an earth filled with mountains, rivers, crystals and animals. In this fourth world we are transitioning out of now, we have encountered complexity, disease and pain. The fourth world is characterised by our collective movement into the heart. And as with any transformational or evolutionary process, the journey is strongest at the end. Transition will bring the centrifuge to its full spin, and then we rise.

In West Africa there is a concept known as Sankofa. Sankofa, in its simplest translation, means looking to the past to be in the moment of now. It is the moment just before we lift our wings, the edge of now and tomorrow. For me, the fifth level brings interculturality and interdependence fully into the conversation. It is a place where our clear looking has been established, we have learned to listen, to feel, and we are truly ready to engage each other as sovereign individuals who are part of a whole.

In this moment we are being born, but we are being born from the heart. And as we are born the wings of the heart lift us, so that we become a collective of birds, flying on currents of love.

The Emergence Legends

There are over 700 tribes across the Americas. These are the indigenous peoples who came, from across the waters, across land bridges, who were present when the great continental split occurred so many, many eons ago. Their stories speak of many migrations. Their stories of coming into existence, or emergence, are even older. They have been passed down through oral tradition for longer than our minds care to comprehend. And while each story is unique to a particular tribe, they share similarities. It has been a great joy of mine to read through as many as possible, to listen to them whenever I've had an opportunity, and to imagine[1].

The first world was watery, dark, barely formed. Viscous air merged with productive waters in a soup of life potential. The desire of love produced the breath and heat of creation. In that spark of the heart sound waves reverberated across time. Those sound waves began to stretch out, across space and space began to unfurl. The first beings lived in the void. We were there, our ancestors, our souls. And we had webbed feet and webbed hands. We must have been less dense, newly formed. We must have breathed with the fullness of our bodies. Our eyes were still waking up. And we were closer to love, to our source. The voice of Creator echoed through our world and through our lives. We swam and we floated. And when it came time to move from this first world into the second, we gathered at a hole in the void. We gathered where the waters and the vapours parted. And we moved up, up through the hole in the void. We opened out into the second world.

The ground of the second world was marshy. The first separation happened between water and air, earth and sky. And we learned to be in the middle, to stretch our arms and legs, to know ourselves within the vast expanse. As the

---

1 These stories have been gathered, absorbed and felt over many years, most of them before I had any idea about how to be a scholar or keep track of sources. My telling of the emergence legends is therefore straight from my heart, which has, with due diligence and attention, given them much respect and contemplation.

world began its first tender separations into various forms of matter, we too separated from our source of love just a little. We came to understand ourselves as configurations in time, in space. Each one of us began to develop our own emergent desire.

In the second world the sky took on many colours. A pale blue rose just near the horizon, a yellow stretched out above it, and finally a brilliant white emerged. Stars came into being and stretched across the expanse. The stars were close to us then, a web of fire we could almost touch. Our sense of wonder and awe was formed. The Sun began to shine upon us. And as we felt warmth cascading over our bodies, the Sun's spark within us began to expand. We moved in beauty, shadow, colour and light. And when it came time to move into the third world, we gathered at the opening in the sky. The heavens parted and we moved through a wave of light onto the ground of the third world.

In the third world mountains arose. In the East mountains arose, in the West mountains arose, in the South mountains arose and in the North mountains arose. We were there and we watched the earth shiver and shake. Water began to move through the mountains. From the great primordial sea the waters rose into the great firmament of sky and began to flow freely through the emerging body of our mother. We experienced rain, and in the mix of fresh and salty waters new forms of life began to form. Many forms of life, flowing out from the imagination and the heart of God. It was a time of prolific creation as the spark of fire in our hearts grew. Our bodies changed, and with these changes we felt the wind. Air caressed our changing skin, we lost hair and gained hair, we felt warmth and we felt cold. We gathered in new ways. And we shared new forms of communication. Tools were created to help us live, arts were created, and all was done slowly, with love, admiration, wonder and care.

In the third world we became masters at dreaming. Our dream life and our waking life merged in a conscious way. Consciousness itself began to know itself. Our separation from love, just a little further, allowed us to look back and to see, to express our longing and our union. So when it came time to move into the fourth world, we considered carefully what to bring with us. The first man and first woman who would move through the smoke hole began to actively dream. They dreamed of movement across the worlds in caravans of families and tribes. They dreamed of invention and flight. They dreamed of gardens laden with an abundance of fruit and flowering vegetation. They dreamed of mountains inset with innumerable crystals and jewels. They dreamed of ritual and the sacred arts. They dreamed a perfect world into being, where we would live forever as goddesses and gods. And when the time came, the people gathered. Singing songs, carrying their blankets and baskets and babies, they gathered where the great smoke hole of the tipi opened. First man and first woman went through the smoke hole first. Then one by one, two by two, ten by ten they migrated into the fourth world. But then – just as the last person was coming through the top of the tipi, that person reached back to grab one more thing. And what they grabbed was not theirs, but that wily coyote's. And so coyote, dashing after what was his, came through the smoke hole into the fourth world with us.

As the people landed on the shores of the fourth world, they began to talk amongst themselves, to sing and to celebrate. They were making magic and using sacred ritual, they were making prayers – when into the gathering came coyote. Coyote was angry that he had not been invited into this world, but found his way here by happenstance. He was upset that he had not had a part in dreaming this world into being and insisted that he now offer something. And because the people knew the ways of coyote, the parts of themselves that he carried, they were worried. Coyote proposed that he throw a stick into the lake. If the stick sank then he would not offer a contribution to this world. If the stick floated, however, he would offer four things to humanity. The people agreed and coyote threw the stick. And of course it floated. So coyote declared that in the fourth world people would carry toothache, lice, ageing and death. He felt that without these things we would become too greedy, too arrogant, too many, too much. Well – discontent and anger arose in the people through the actions of coyote, and these have been with us ever since, even though his actions did carry some wisdom with them.

As we move from the fourth world into the fifth, we have a choice about what we bring. This moment of chaos we are in – it precedes our gathering and movement. And through it, we are letting go. By the beauty of a bigger momentum, we have gifted ourselves time and space to reflect deeply on our hearts. For the heart is the steep, the mountaintop, the launching pad by which we will migrate from the fourth to the fifth world. What wisdom have we gained in the heart. What will our choices be?

Thomas Banyacya (1909–1999), an elder of the Hopi Nation, began to share the wisdom of his oral tradition with outsiders during the later stages of his life. He speaks across time of the worlds we have moved through. And according to Banyacya, human life on Earth has been almost fully destroyed preceding each movement. The nature of our human condition, which is both the beauty and the terror of our free will, has more than once failed to stay in a place of reciprocity and balance with the planet (1995). Through each movement, however, across each world and through time, consciousness is evolving. As God, love, Allah comes to know his/herself in more and more detail, our spiritual and personal power grows.

Perhaps the most symbolic representation of emergence is the rainbow. The rainbow is circular, full of every spectrum of colour. The rainbow appears after the chaos, after the storm. The rainbow carries the twinkling eyes of our ancestors and makes a bridge across the heavens. And I don't know about you, but I've seen an awful lot of rainbows in people's windows these past few years.

Level Six: Vision

The sixth level is the fire of transmutation. Connected to the pineal gland and centre of the brain, it is the highest centre of thought and feeling in the body, where information from the cosmos meets the human imagination. The sixth centre brings clarity and precision to our being, to our lives. It is where the waters and emotion of the lower centres, having been burned and purified in the heart, having found expression in the fifth centre, then rise to the heavens. It is the centre of imagination. When we are aligned to a place of pure love, our imaginations are filled with goodness. The capacity to imagine a world of beauty truly unfolds. It is through development of the sixth centre that we have the opportunity to leave the karma we have created behind. When we apply structure to the dreaming of the visionary eye, there is no limit to what we can create. It is a place where cooperation becomes something beautiful. For while we remain centred in lower levels cooperation can feel difficult. For example, it is difficult to process a lot of emotion together, and to activate our collective willpower from a place of love rather than fear. But if we have all aligned to love, cooperation becomes a tool for our passion. Thus the attributes of forgiveness and compassion, rising from the heart, meet clear communication in the fifth centre, and the energies of fresh birth in the sixth.

The sixth centre is located in the middle of the forehead, at the centre of the brow. The sixth centre is associated with the colour purple, with dreaming and with structure. It is sometimes known as the third eye or the visionary eye.

Visionary Fire

As we enter a fresh birth, our need for new structures will, out of necessity, push us into collaboration and community. Changes in how we exchange services and goods will result from our needs for local trade. Through these changes communities will be born. And if we understand that there are skills we can bring to the table, our communities have a chance of thriving. These skills involve structures we have forgotten about, structures relating to dreaming, communication, council, decision making and love. For example, in the Iroquois Confederacy of six nations, which includes six different tribes of the Great Lakes region of North America, dreaming and decision-making have traditionally been intertwined. Each morning, the people would wake early, bathe in the river and gather. Time was taken to listen to the dreams they had been given in the night. And decisions for the day were based upon what had been revealed. Further, councils of all six tribes were regularly held. At these councils, the elders would officiate. They would bring all information to bear, including the messages of nature. Toward the end of the council, proposed changes and plans were brought before the grandmothers. And the grandmothers made the final decision on all matters. These structures are simple. They are based in reciprocity with the dreamtime, with each other and with nature. These structures hold the life-giving presence of the womb and her wisdom, as she matures, as the vital power behind collective action.

In terms of love, we can look to the vastness and depth of our spiritual traditions to supply many useful spiritual technologies. These technologies are tools for the journey of the human through their development and spiritual maturity. They involve practices such as mantra, chanting, fasting, music, dance and prayer. A deep study of human psychology, nature and the universe accompany almost every tradition. And these technologies bring us fully into the presence of love. They bring us structures whereby our communities may reside together with love indwelling in the heart. While the present moment and the future will never look exactly like the past, we can look to the past to inform our present choices. For the ancestors and the elders have passed these technologies and tools down to us, generation after generation, with deep care. And if we are wise, we will harness them so that we too may pass a better world on to our own children.

The magnificent, fractal nature of existence can be more fully embodied by us here on Earth. Through the use of sacred tools such as geometry and mathematics we might make visible the deeper knowledges of our universe within our daily lives. Through the use of sacred technologies such as sound and breath, we might make whole our cycles of food production and waste management. Through the use of sacred languages such as astronomy and navigation, we might open whole new vistas of transportation and communications. The way I am grouping our tools and possibilities might seem a little crazy; however, there is a good deal of subtle information underlining my choices. The discoveries and inventions of the visionary eye are extraordinary to perceptions rooted in the fourth world. They are, however, founded on principles. And these principles are readily available to a different type of knowing – a knowing that finds a resting place within centres such as the visionary eye. From the tiniest fern frond to the movements of the galaxies, the visionary eye has different methods for retrieving and processing that information. The nature of the universe is holographic. And the wider information of the universe will be useful to us as we create new ways of life. These new life ways will require, or engender, a mind-blowing combination of our sciences, arts and spiritual technologies. So a whole new level of cooperation will be required in the fifth world. And it is the visionary sixth centre, the fiery third eye, that will help us negotiate these complex cooperations. Like the philosopher's stone, only humans who are living fully in the heart will be able to manifest it. And we are those humans.

So how do we get there? Structures like to be put into action, and it is time we apply our power to dream. Right now, we are being called to be our own heroes, to trust ourselves, and to allow for a diversity of responses to the present situation. Right now, we do not need to agree on what is happening in order to take charge of our sovereignty. We only need to trust the feeling that something is changing, something is in need of doing, and that we each have a vital part to play in creating a different outcome. Each heart now has the universal momentum and support to find its home. And together we can create solutions that work for our capacities, our environment as it is. There is no right or wrong here. There is only a moment of conflagration where diverse agendas have a meeting point. At this meeting point the heat and friction, the energy we need for transformation, are present. When we take full responsibility for our present predicament – and start looking to inner rather than outer power to solve it – we begin to build a way out of it and forward.

Purity and Purification
Fire purifies. And just as fire is located in the third centre, as we ignite our willpower, fire is also present in the sixth centre. Here at the top, the fire is of a spiritual nature, less animal. The fire is more refined.

For a hive to work together effectively, each member must be whole within themselves. Not every bee needs to be a superstar – in fact quite the opposite is true. Each bee needs only to live its own capacities fully. And if we consider the 99, or infinite, qualities of God that are embodied across the billions of us on the planet, then we can see the importance of each bee, each human, each star shining in just its own way[2]. When each of us is born, we have certain lessons or paths that we must journey on our individual way to wholeness. No two paths are exactly the same. So if we are gentle with each other, allowing for the natural growth to blossom for each person, in their own time and their own way, we will eventually come to a wholeness. This level of inclusivity takes a broad look at evolution and time, and it is useful to us. I see this level of inclusivity as a lived reality within the Sufi communities I am part of. And it is true, it works. The glue that holds such a community together is a shared recognition of the importance of purity and purification.

Purification is a continual process. We take a shower each day to wash our skin. Why then would we not wash our hearts, our minds and our emotions? Further, our energy bodies – which are formed of the electromagnetic signals which extend from our hearts, mind and emotions – love a regular dusting and feathering. We are slowly beginning to remember or to recognise this. Meditation for example, is a good bath for the mind. Exercise and yoga move the fluids of our system so that our physical heart and blood have a chance to cleanse themselves. Practices such as The Emotional Freedom Technique and Access Bars are very simple and helpful for regularly washing the emotions. So is a good cry. And a good laugh. Dancing brings the mind, body and emotions into the shower together. And music moves us to dance. So we see that the spiritual technologies have a very grounded root. When we as communities are attended to purification we are able to live life in a sacred manner without becoming overly serious. We set aside time for ritual, for deeper cleansing. This cleansing becomes part of our structures, and all benefit.

Level Seven: Jewel of the Universe

Level seven is that of the crown. It is the soft spot at the top of the head in babies. It is the image of the lotus flower in bloom in the Indian and Vedic traditions. It is the place where the soul enters during the embryonic stage of our formation. And it is the spot where the heart is formed as well. The first flexion of the foetus in the womb serves to migrate the heart from the top of the head into the torso. So the cellular blueprint of the heart and the crown are one and the same[3]. The crown is the space where the complete human being is realised.

---

2 The 99 names of God represent 99 qualities that we commonly see embodied in the human form. Each of us is a unique combination of embodiments. No two humans are ever completely alike. And as God is present equally in all aspects of manifestation, God is only fully existent when we are all exactly who we are.

3 I learned this magnificent aspect of embryology at a conference many years ago. The

The one who witnesses and the one who knows are one and the same. The one who both receives and emits love, who is united with God, Allah, Great Spirit in every moment. The crown is a space where inner and outer harmony are manifest. The space of the crown is subtle, refined. Its expression is that of beauty and it is a fountain of grace.

Hazrat Inayat Khan, founder of the Chisti Order of Sufis in India, writes,

The reach of vibrations is according to the fineness of the plane of their starting-point. To speak more plainly, the word uttered by the lips can only reach the ears of the hearer; but the thought proceeding from the mind reaches far, shooting from mind to mind. The vibrations of mind are much stronger than those of words. The earnest feelings of one heart can pierce the heart of another; they speak in the silence, spreading out into the sphere, so that the very atmosphere of a person's presence proclaims his thoughts and emotions. The vibrations of the soul are the most powerful and far-reaching, they run like an electric current from soul to soul. (1996)

So the crown is the seat of the soul. In Sufism, the Earth is seen as the jewel of the entire universe. The love that we generate here moves in waves through the whole of all creation. We are the generators of love, and all of creation benefits when we carry love in our hearts. When we have become sufficiently mature, when our structures support a true spiritual love to flow between us in community and harmony, then that love rises to the crown. Then that love is known by God, it is returned to its home and the impulse of creation is fulfilled. The desire for God, love, Allah to know him/herself is fully circular and whole in that moment. And this is our destiny, if we choose it. At each epoch of change, we are again presented with this opportunity. Both individually and collectively, for creation is holographic. And the compassion of divine love ensures that eventually it comes home to itself. If we live to see it *en masse,* wonderful. And if not, then perhaps our children or grandchildren or great, great, great, great grandchildren will embody our collective return. In truth, it is embodied by some of us at all times.

---

speaker was a Dutch embryologist and he had intrauterine footage of the migration. It was so fascinating that is has stayed with me all these years. I do not remember his name.

As this space is subtle there is less that can be communicated in words. Music is the most appropriate to share the vibrations of this centre, and according to Khan, forms a foundation of any golden age. One thing to share, however, is that in reaching the seventh centre life does not automatically become a golden utopia. To live and embody a golden age is a state of grace, a state of allowing. This means that all qualities of the earthly plane are still present. What is different is that the golden river of unity flows through. Anger may rise, sadness may rise, hunger or separation or cold may rise; however, they flow through. And once again we are in the river. Always aware of the river. With every rise and fall of an epoch, our witness and knowledge and appreciation of the river of unity matures. God comes to know him/herself at ever new and deepening layers. And that happens through us. Through the sincere and beautiful and willing nature of our hearts. For love is infinite, and expansion has no beginning and no end.

The Seven Levels: Some Main Points

We are part of a bigger picture. There is a river moving through time. In epoch after epoch, life on this planet may extend back further than we care to imagine. Consciousness is ever evolving, and at this moment in time we are at a global and collective juncture.

Life has a value. Life itself is what is at stake in this moment. And we can learn from the past to make better choices for our present and our future.

Regarding our responses to this great moment of conflagration, it is clear that the effects of war and the removal of civil liberties will not offer our best solutions. As human bodies and beings, we know how to heal each other, to heal ourselves, to heal the earth and to create a new society. We only need to remember.

If we are to survive, we must take back power over our own food production, education and housing. Our natural spaces are important. A natural education is important. And life begins with planting seeds so that we can eat. It is time we stop putting the interests of an economic structure above our imperative to foster the continuation of life.

Similarly, it is absolutely necessary that we take back power and responsibility over our own healthcare. Everything we need is provided by the Earth, and many skilled healers exist around the planet. Let them lead us, let them teach us, and let us receive this wisdom with grace. While Western medicine has had many advances, it depends on synthetic manufacture of harmful substances and is tied to the trauma of surgery. The technologies that may be born when we open our hearts and minds to their possibility will move far beyond what we currently call advances. But this is a process that involves true healing on the deepest of levels. It involves taking responsibility for ourselves and caring for each other deeply from the very outset of our lives.

Our hearts are opening and our hearts know their truth. Every child and person has both a right and a duty to pursue what their heart burns and yearns for – to be part of a wider whole and contribute the fullness of their own unique quality.

Finally, we are all opening to the beauty and necessity of compassion and care. It is simply not acceptable that some should go without while others have so much more than they need. And here I am talking about clean water and clean air as much as about material goods – about beauty and belonging as much as shelter and food. It is not helpful to look to government to regulate this for us, for the interest of government is to profit itself. We can regulate and mature ourselves. We can, with awareness and choice, enter the space of the heart again. Where the subtle and material meet, we can dwell in purity and sincerity, for the health of our own families, communities, and for everyone on the planet.

Can we forgive ourselves for what we have already allowed to happen? Can we be compassionate with ourselves for giving away our sovereignty? Can we love ourselves enough to forgive each other for the monstrous things we have witnessed? Can we gather our inner resources to come together with humbleness and dream a better way forward? I believe we can. I believe we are spiritually supported at this moment in time to do so. And I believe it is the only viable response to the moment.

In the next chapters I will bring many of the aspects presented here into fuller detail and context. Through beautiful stories, spiritual teachings and thoughtful consideration, we may be inspired to our own truth and the direction that it calls us to.

Part 2

Chapter Three

The Divine Feminine

The divine feminine is a term that is just coming into the public consciousness at large. It is being defined as we awaken, for we are in a process of discovery. When we look at the bigger picture of time we see that there have been many epochs of human life upon this planet, many worlds that we have embodied. Within each world have been cycles of growth, apex, decline, transition, rising and then another apex. Ways of life have sustained themselves and then fallen away, giving up themselves for the next wave of consciousness as it develops. And within these ways of life there have been cultures of both matriarchy and patriarchy. For instance, there is a teaching among the North American indigenous peoples of a time when women had cherished their positions as keepers of the sacred knowledges, but had then fallen away from the very truths they embodied and espoused. So for a time the men became the keepers of the sacred ways and the women went through a process of decline, choice and rebirth (Moon, 1984).

The moment we are in now comes at the end of an age of patriarchy. During this age we have seen ourselves give power to forces such as slavery, war and greed. We have chosen to dominate rather than cooperate, and we are seeing the end of the road that these choices have led to. And as much good, culture and art has transpired within this age, we now have no way to continue life within the paradigm of patriarchy we have lived for the last few thousands of years. This juncture of our consciousness aligns with a new planetary position for Earth within our galaxy. The Earth is spinning not only around itself, but through space, and as we do so we are continually arriving at a new solar relationship between the Earth and Sun. In the solar relationship we now find ourselves in, there is more support for the feminine energies of Earth to be seen, felt and lived[1].

---

1 The mathematical relationship of Earth, Sun and orbit has been written about extensively in the Vedas. For a thorough contemporary reading of it see Yukteswar (1948). And for application of these principles in the Americas see Clow (2007).

As the feminine energies naturally rise, we as women are beginning to remember the truths we carry in our blood, our wombs, our bones. Just as there is no new water upon the planet, for it cycles continuously through sky, earth and ocean, there is no new matter. Our bones hold the memories of our ancestors. And our wombs carry the knowledge of ages past, beyond the written word and civilisations of this epoch.

Since I was a young child I have had dreams of ancient rites and ways of different matriarchal cultures. I had no way to place or understand them until I began to read stories confirming my experience. More recently, the culture at large has begun to speak of the same things. As I grew into my own maturity, I found not only written but also embodied accounts that give meaning to the life of my dreams. In this particular text, it is not my intention to cover all the ways a powerful feminine leadership might look. It is rather my intention to bring discussions of the divine feminine into conversations around our issues of transition. As we meet the intersecting points of various possibilities, each one of us must discover for ourselves where the truth lives within them. In this chapter I offer thoughts from indigenous and spiritual knowledges as well as from the various paths that I carry. The rising feminine energies have a place in the choices and changes we each now face. To bring them in with awareness will help us greatly. As for the divine aspect to the conversation, we are each divine – male, female and all genders. As feminine energies rise, the very sacred role of women within the life continuum will come forward. While feminine qualities will rise within all of us, we may as a species rediscover the act of birth as a divine rite, privilege and sacrifice. Alongside this a divine masculine will be reborn. And in the coming age we have an opportunity to co-embody divine truths as not a matriarchy or a patriarchy, but as a balanced human consciousness rooted to love and God. And the first step is a natural redress of the patriarchy as we have recently lived it. As the pendulum swings, the feminine is emerging.

The Feminine Principle

Life on Earth is a plane of duality, meaning that opposite energies swirl around each other and in so doing, meeting points occur whereby creation happens. One of the most obvious pairs of opposites within the earthly realm is that of masculine and feminine. Prior to or underneath the stories we carry of our own femininity, let us look at it as a principle. The feminine principle as a set of universal archetypes moves through all of us, male and female, and may be realised within everyone.

To what degree we each cultivate a natural feminine/masculine balance through our lived experience is a matter of our unique manifestation. That we all have the ability, and the need, to recognise and develop both qualities is certain. And this can be accomplished no matter the biology. A woman with a womb still needs to honour the masculine within her. A man with a penis still needs to honour the feminine within him. The outer dress and appearance are much less important than the inner qualities of each principle.

Reciprocity, surrender, courage, resilience and care are foundations of the feminine principle. Qualities of receptivity, circularity and the giving of space/allowing are equally important. The feminine principle is related to night, to the Moon, to timelessness, darkness, the energy that supplies life – which brings us out of the dark and into form. A reciprocity between birth and death, a surrender to both processes, and the resilience needed to encounter them define the feminine principle. Attention to detail, and the care that is engendered by this, is also feminine.

As a foundation of the feminine principle, reciprocity rests central. Within that is a need to receive as deeply as ones gives. The Earth naturally gives up fruit for her children. In giving, she receives. And this relationship between giving and receiving is a natural part of reciprocity. Likewise, the mother gives up her body for her children. In giving, she receives – her own flesh, life and heart are recreated. Reciprocity has at its core care. A deep care, related to love, moves a mother to nurse and tend to another woman's child. A deep care, related to love, moves a human to nurse and tend to another species. A deep care, related to love, moves heaven and earth to ensure equality and safety for all, be they plant, animal or human. Over the last hundreds and thousands of years, reciprocity has gone further and further missing in the patriarchal renditions of familial, spiritual and social living. As the church has denigrated and subverted the feminine, the male of a family was until recently – legally allowed to beat and abuse his wife and children. At least in the West. In some parts of the world this is still the case. And in the private hearts and homes of many, the hurdles we have toward a recognition, care and devotion to the feminine are still massive. How we handle bodies, and people, who are vulnerable is part of our social fabric.

For womb-man, reciprocity is not an ideology. It is a part of the birth process at a survival level. Through modern medicine, women have been separated from the process of birth, so much so that our births are often chemically induced, scheduled and subjected to so many interventions that the mother may not even be cognisant. In such circumstances the mother has given away her power to bring life into the world on her own terms. She has given up her freedoms of choice, and in so doing she has forgotten her sacred role in her culture. Without woman and mother at the centre, there is imbalance, to the degree that life itself is no longer certain for our species. For the way we care for our life-giving processes reflects the way we care for the Earth. As woman is giver of life, so is the Earth giver of life. The feminine principle relates as well to the soil and the body of terra firma. The attention, tenderness and reciprocity we afford to the Earth is a direct reflection of how we relate to the feminine within. This is not an essentialised statement, but rather a recognition that it is only through the bodies of women and the soil of this earth that life exists on this planet at all. And that is all life – animal, fish, bird, plant and human.

As women, we have accepted the denigration of our qualities and physical bodies. In many cases, we have even been the ones to denigrate and shame. The rising of the feminine is a task not just for men to embrace. As women, we must face the uncomfortable place of equal participation in our subjugation. As humans, we are called to nurture and develop the archetypal qualities of the feminine in both our inner and our outer lives.

There is a wealth of discovery to be made surrounding the feminine principle. It is receptive, watery, dark. It is the salty water of the oceans, which are akin to the saline waters of the womb. It is the fresh waters of the rivers, which are akin to our joy and tears. The feminine is strong like the rock and mountains of the Earth. She is ever giving, in her cycles of death and rebirth, of autumn and spring. The feminine is a powerful protector and defender of the young. She is the guardian and custodian of the human heart. The feminine has a need for rest as much as activity. And she is social, co-existing with other energies in reciprocity. The feminine is a solution finder not by logic, but by wisdom. She is intuition. She is grace. And the feminine is part of all of us.

If we want to revivify and make new the feminine within ourselves as a species, then it is in our interest to become a part of living nature. To touch the earth, soil, stars and sky, to become part of the moving waters. To harmonise a lived, shared connection, to bodies and the body of the Earth. When we connect to the life-giving power of the female biology, to all that it represents, then we once again begin to value our presence upon the planet. We are not parasites upon the Earth, but her very children. We exist out of her grace and giving. And when we honour the Earth as our collective mother, there is enough and abundance for all. We can learn, as humans, to honour female bodies and the Earth as the living potentiality of creation. Without the generations of women past there is no life in the present moment. Without the women who give birth now, where will the life of the future come from?

Archetypes of Femininity

As we look to the archetypes of femininity and their movements within life – imprinted by psychology, environment and experience – we then open a conversation on balance. For the feminine in balance is a perfect outpouring of her principles. Out of balance, however, there are common distortions, and these are important to recognise. As we look at the feminine in her more varied expressions, we offer our attention so that she may heal and rise to her feet, taking a place of leadership in the paradigm being born. And just as the feminine has a shadow and a light, so does the masculine. For a woman to be in total balance within, the masculine principle must also be integrated. In balance, the masculine principle is warm, forward-moving, generous and kind. Out of balance the masculine is dominant, overpowering and egotistically driven. When a healthy, divine masculine and feminine principle work together in harmony, an incredible light-filled beacon may then emerge for the benefit of all.

The raging feminine is an aspect of the unhealed feminine that most of us are familiar with. If you are a woman, you have felt it. And if you are a man, you have probably experienced it at the behest of a mother or a partner, or in the collective as a backlash to the patriarchy. There is a well of grief and rage within women that needs expression. And women benefit from a masculine energy to witness and hold that expression so that it may move through to its transformation. Let's look at where this rage comes from.

For thousands of years of women have been routinely sold into marriages, have had no control over how many children they birth or how often. Women have upheld the work of a household completely on their own, and in many cases have been submitted to routine rape and violence at the behest of husbands and family members. And in some places, women have also undergone customary mutilation. In the worst conditions, women are sold as sexual objects for the profit and survival of the larger family. None of this has been acceptable. Women, as humans, have basic rights over their own bodies, and should always have the say over when they engage sexually, with whom, when they birth children, with whom and how. Women, as humans, have a basic right to feel and know love. They have a basic right to livelihood, pursuit of improvement and education. And for so, so many, all of this has been denied. So as the feminine awakens collectively within the human family, there is much to be seen, felt, heard and released.

The raging feminine is the archetype that has felt too much, seen too much, and has been left without a voice for too long. In the work that I do with women, I see the raging feminine surface with tears and anguish, with guilt and often with confusion. She knows that she needs to be seen in her pain, yet does not always have an appropriate outlet for that witness. And when this is the case, she will blame, scoff and rage at her partner, her family and the culture at large. And as difficult as she may be in these expressions, she is right to do so, for she is simply doing her best to voice that which is unexpressible. If we as a culture truly desire balance and peace, then we must make peace with the raging feminine within us. We must see her, feel her, and allow her the space she needs to move through the wounding she has suffered. Even just a small amount of presence and kindness can do wonders for the raging feminine when she appears, and point her in the direction of freedom.

The contriving or manipulative feminine is another archetype that emerges from the underwater of the feminine as she surfaces. The manipulative or contriving feminine tends to see her world from the place of trauma. From this perspective, individuals, situations and the culture at large are not to be trusted without proof, as they are potential threats. Having experienced so much shame and pain, the manipulative feminine becomes cold, calculating. She sabotages her relationships. She does not trust. And she is ever on the watch, waiting for danger to appear, working to subvert it before it can hurt her yet again.

For a woman who has suffered too much, or who has seen her mother, sisters or in-laws suffer greatly, the protectress has become distorted. Having no solid ground, or safe experience to stand on, the contriving feminine lashes out in deeply harmful ways to those around her. The complexity of the psyche in women who find themselves in this place is profound. It can take a vast amount of care, witness and reassurance to bring through a basic sense of safety. And then a period of opportunity is needed. The opportunity for education, for a livelihood of her own, for comradeship and community are vital. The contriving feminine will test the fresh waters again and again, and it takes a strong, whole masculine to hold this testing. That holding can be done by any human, recognising that it is the healthy masculine principle of generosity, care and right action that will ameliorate the manipulative feminine. Women: we can embody these masculine qualities for ourselves and for each other. At the end of the day, it is not our partners' or our communities' job to continually hold and reassure us. It is our job, and we have the power to embody the fullness of all the principles we need within us. For the health of our communities, as well as ourselves, it is vital that we learn to do so.

In our most recent decades the competitive feminine has had the limelight. Stemming from a place where men had many wives, and if they were wealthy also concubines, the feminine has learned to work against her sisters to secure the life she has a basic right to. The inherent space of womanhood is sisterhood, where we support each other through our blood and menstrual cycles, we assist each other in childbirth and childrearing, we affirm each other and celebrate each others' beauty. To this day, women in Eastern and Middle Eastern culture still gather regularly to beautify, uplift and care for each other. Sisterhoods of women who find this life-affirming space are strong, and their entire communities are stronger for it. Sadly, in every part of the world, many women seek a sisterhood but do not find it.

When a sister steals the partner of another, puts down or goes behind the back of her own friend, or sets herself up as better, a deep rift is formed. A rift that is unnatural and harmful to women on both sides of the action. As women, it is only ourselves who can heal this great wound. It is up to us to celebrate each other, care for and look out for each other. It is up to us to refuse to harm each other any further, and then to educate our men and our society. First we educate our sons and our partners. We start with our own home and when we are ready, we shine an example to the wider community. We educate our sons and our men through self-belief and by example. As they witness our deep care for ourselves and our sisterhood, they will see in action what is good and appropriate. For many of our men do not have examples of empowered women in their lives. Once we are able to live by example, and while we are learning, we go a step further by communicating honestly and from our hearts. There is nothing in this world that can touch the heart of a man or child more than the open, loving communication of a woman and a mother.

The empowered feminine may then emerge as a body of women who know the pain that they have suffered, who know the shadows of rage and competition, and who choose to embrace the full light and love of their own inner resources, of their own hearts. The empowered feminine is able to be receptive and soft whilst remaining firm. She understands that boundaries are hers to define and to communicate. And she trusts that she has the inner power and outer support to do so. She is not afraid to speak, to move powerfully in the world. And she is free to do so with a soft yet clear voice. A voice that commands respect and expects to receive it. Her grace is astounding, and she celebrates her own beauty and the beauty of all women, of all life, with incredible vigour and ease.

Feminisms

We can now move into a brief conversation on feminism, because it is important. Feminism has laid a foundation in the collective mind that allows for expression and steering of the rising feminine energy we are now experiencing. And feminism may have a lot to offer on issues such as nuclear disarmament, healthy food production, fair housing and clean water for all. To put such concerns through a lens of feminism asks us to include the female experience as foundational to our new solutions. And this step, this perceptual shift, is necessary if our solutions are to last long term and to serve us for the next generations.

Feminism has had several waves across the 20th century. As a concept feminism began and has been centred for the most part in Europe and North America. As feminism has developed, its reach has continued to expand and widen. In the beginning, women simply wanted a voice, in governance and in their homes.

They fought for this, banding together, to stand for the value of their own minds and the relevance of their opinions. Many suffered, some even died – for example in the hunger strikes of the suffragettes. The first wave was the only possible step at the time. And it was an important step. Later, women began to crave not just a voice but true freedom. We desired freedom over our own bodies, the choice to have children or not, and we craved financial freedom, the ability to earn and to use our own income. This too was important, and many women fought tirelessly for reproductive and economic equality. At the present moment, most Western women now have access to gynaecological healthcare as well as birth control – if they choose to use it. We are able to pursue education and employment of our choosing, and it is acceptable for us to ask for equal pay, though it is still not always given.

I am a woman who has grown up with this basic voice, healthcare and privilege to education and work. From the vantage point of my lived reality, it is ridiculous to think that we were ever denied these basic rights. The amount of thought, debate, public speaking, protest, action and eventually legislation that has been required to ensure these rights for myself and my generation is phenomenal. And I thank the women who have come before me, working together, to create the conditions that I live so freely in now. And as much as I celebrate the freedoms we have won, I also feel incredulous that we ever had to fight to begin with. When I look beyond my own circumstance, I see so much oppression and repression still happening. Here in the West I see the body shame of our daughters, a collective confusion about healthy sexual boundaries and rape, and the intimidating forces of patriarchal domination in the financial sector. When I look to other cultures, I see that forced marriage, genital mutilation and lack of basic gynaecological healthcare are still problems. I see education and independent livelihood as realities that not all women yet have access to. And when I look from the space of my feeling, I see that the freedoms we have gained have not yet led to true freedom for our hearts. I see that the Earth and our hearts are not yet held in sacred trust, and that they are still crying. And I am not the only one. In terms of a healthy, empowered feminine and a lived reality of the feminine principle within the collective, we have a long way to go. Thus we have contemporary and new waves of feminism now brewing.

Twenty-first century feminism can be seen to take up the mantle of inclusivity, reciprocity and care. The inclusion of children and other minority voices has become important. The voice of the heart is wanting witness. And the ties of womanhood to earth and her crisis point are becoming apparent.

Contemporary feminism engages advancing thought in sexual difference, nomadism, ecofeminism, gender and transgender issues. It can be seen publicly in movements such as #MeToo, a global drive to bring light to the freedom of sexual innocence for young women and children, especially those who are a part of the entertainment industry. There is also the Dove Real Beauty campaign, which encourages critique of unnatural beauty standards which create ill health and suffering in all. Further examples include movements such as #ShoutOutToTheNight, where women speak publicly of their stories of rape and molestation on platforms to public audiences. They are given emotional and practical support, lighting, microphones, and cultural recognition. Also The Vagina Monologues, where women perform on stage the stories, yearnings and pleasures of their own bodies, in their own voices. And finally #HeForShe, a global project that aims to help individuals engage achievable, simple methods of gender equality in their lives, thus opening conversations and creating ripples within the collective psyche. Such examples show that feminism is moving into mainstream thought. Our new waves of feminism are as important as the first ones, for their gains will impact us as deeply, and they spiral one step closer to the heart.

Slowly, with care, the waves of feminism as they have moved across the 20th and now 21st centuries are bringing a minority voice, the voice of the feminine, into the majority. And this is creating change, in small communities across towns and villages worldwide. Mothers are standing up against genital mutilation of their daughters in Africa. Mothers are speaking out against paedophilia in schools, churches and institutions. Mothers are encouraging their daughters to feel beautiful at any size, with or without makeup. And our daughters and granddaughters will likely feel that it was barbaric to have ever had to stand up for ourselves in this way at all. Thank God for that.

When we look at the lives of real women, across the planet, there is much diversity, which is in large part due to the weights and levers that the first three waves of feminism have rebalanced. These lives include women who have children and who choose not to have children; women who work and women who raise families full time – as well as women who do both; women who are part of large and intricate family structures and women who create a family of simply themselves. Within this milieu of diversity multiple new strains of feminism are taking root, each important. One of these strains is known as 'the project of sexual difference' (Braidotti, 2011).

The project of sexual difference seeks to harmonise both the biology of womb-men, which is without end or limitation, as well as key qualities of the feminine inter-culturally. These qualities would include subjectivity, multiplicity, cooperative and non-hierarchical structures, as well as values such as beauty, rest and spaciousness. The project of sexual difference gives voices to the biological power of the womb and the vagina – while allowing for the multiplicity of ways a woman (and human) may choose to identify themselves. Recognising the power it takes to carry a child, give birth, nurse and nurture that child while rearing a family and maintaining a household, often while working – woman is recognised in her strength. And this strength is not only physical but emotional. And it is this emotional strength that brings forward missing and necessary aspects to our worlds of commerce and civilisation. It is from the diverse, multidimensional reality of womanhood that diverse, multilayered solutions to our present social and cultural dilemmas may begin to form. And as woman is centred in the sphere of her own body, especially while having and rearing children, so will feminine solutions be centred in the local. As women begin to honour their own inner logic and rewrite their stories, we become beacons of power and hope. We become goddesses. And a true goddess is one who inspires and gives life to a civilisation or a paradigm or ontology. In this way our biological truths might influence, and inspire, worlds and lives far beyond the biological starting point.

A core, lived truth of millions of women globally is the life-giving and life-affirming reality of being one who births children, of being one who has a womb and recognises it as a centre of power. However, women do not always choose to have physical children. Through their creative power, women may birth many wonderful things into this world. These might include projects such as orphanages, refugee homes, reforestation and environmental initiatives, educational reforms, new books, new music, charities, new scientific discoveries, legal and human rights advances, business and entrepreneurship, or just plain mentorship of the neighbourhood kids or elderly. The productive power of womb-man is endless. It seeks not to promote itself solely, but to expand itself within the lives of others, within hearts and through community. When we recognise this truth, projects of sexual difference can sit comfortably alongside other contemporary shoots of feminism. For the truth is we are not just one strain of woman. We are multiple, diamond shaped prisms of endless rainbow colours.

There is something to say about branches of feminism that seek to emphasise inclusion, especially gender inclusion, as their core. This sense of inclusion, which is a feminine quality, embraces the rising feminine energies as they express across genders. And it is important. For the feminine energies, as they move into global consciousness, are becoming embodied by all. This is indicative of a change from a patriarchal age and over-culture to an equanimous age where male and female are balanced. The inclusive branches of feminism do not need to stand in opposition to an equally important project of sexual difference. Each brings forward a river of truth which is vital. And in their meeting, these two rivers make peace with the earliest and most detrimental rift of first wave feminism. And that is the debate about whether or not woman is 'essentialised'[2].

Here I wish to bring light again to the womb. The womb not only exists, it is the only way any being – human, mammal or bird – has come into existence on this planet. We are not yet born in petri dishes, and we may decide, when the time comes, that it is not such a good idea to produce ourselves in labs. We may come to understand that the very existence and continuation of life

---

2 Early French feminism brought the essential nature of woman to the forefront, celebrating her relationship to the Earth and to the feminine principle. Subsequent waves of feminism rallied against that, especially as they fought for equal recognition in the workplace and patriarchal paradigms. In the 'project of sexual difference' I see a resolution to this early rift, indicative of the widening ways women are interrogating and celebrating their inner worlds.

rests on our ability to bring peace to the body of woman. We will hold both the creative power of the feminine and women choosing to birth human life as sacred. As we do this, we will understand that such a move does not exclude the feminine, she rises in every gender. We will meet at a lagoon where different but similar rivers touch, in celebration of life, harmony and diversity, all grounded in the feminine.

Ecofeminism

Within the panorama of feminist movements and sub-movements rests a beautiful gem known as ecofeminism.

Ecofeminism began emerging through individual women as early as 1974. Linking ecology and feminism, ecofeminism seeks to redress a lack of balance in our relationship to the Earth. The roles women play in stewarding and protecting the Earth and her beings, animals and children, are foundational to ecofeminism. The sentience and basic rights of all beings are viewed as interconnected to the ecology and health of the planet – in culture, society, the family and our personal lives. For me, a real strength of ecofeminism is its emphasis on practical matters. Ecofeminism takes a long and critical look at issues such as healthcare, housing, food supply and education. For while we may theoretically speak to discrimination and violence, it is our grounded actions that provide reprieve. While we write and inquire, it is important that we help lift the very real burdens many women's bodies are bearing[3]. My own heart, in its inner inquiry, has often sought deep redress for women, children and all beings who are victims of violence and subversion. Witnessing the exploitation of our Earth and her resources, at a cost to her health and ability to thrive, it is not difficult to make a link between how we treat the bodies of women and the body of the Earth. It therefore makes a lot of sense to extend the sentience and basic set rights we have fought for in feminism to the Earth herself. In healing the collective body of women on the planet, we also heal and restore the body of the Earth, and vice versa.

I personally feel that ecofeminism has an important role to play in our emerging, new ways of life. An elder who has been patiently waiting her time to speak, ecofeminism may take fresh inspiration from her younger sisters. As

---

3 For me, the privilege of inquiry and theoretical engagement signposts my colonial heritage. Through the capitalist structures that have allowed me to live in comfort and ease, women and families worldwide have suffered. The expense they have paid is still not recognised enough, and there is still much to be done to disentangle ourselves from the far-reaching effects of patriarchy within globalism.

our climate adjusts to both longitudinal geological change and the impact of recent civilisation – and we in turn adjust to our Earth's responses – we will of necessity become sober with ourselves, our choices. We will begin to perceive the Earth as sentient, and our survival dependent on an inherent reciprocity with her. We will come to recognise collectively that the body of the Earth and the body of women are inextricably linked. And thus our policies will change. Our structures will change. What is today normalised will, looking back, be seen yet again as barbaric. And so, without being unduly riotous, this is a message of hope for all of us. A message to say keep feeling into what your hearts are saying, what your own wombs and the wombs that you were carried in are speaking. See how far your inclusivity can stretch and how deeply your care might imprint the greater whole. For as individuals, you will impact greater cultural change – it is only a matter of time. And the deeper we feel, the more we bring our hearts and our bodies together, the better we are able to act upon our inner truth and to support each other. This is turn creates a unified heart field between us, a voice of beauty which is indicative of a maturing feminine. This is a voice which can only grow.

The Western Woman

The Dalai Lama has said that 'Western woman will change the world' (Chan, 2010). As a Western woman, this is a statement I have really looked at. It is not unproblematic. As a Western woman myself, I am very aware of my privilege. I am sincere in my own heart, yet part of a larger mechanism. I have struggles of my own which are often difficult to bear, yet my privilege cannot be ignored. I look to women and to mothers across the world and I feel my heart expanded, connected. But I also feel pain and commiseration. I consider, 'What is our responsibility?'. For it is the West that has colonised and culturally stripped more than half the planet. It is the West that created debt and a monetary system reliant on dependency. It is the West that spread a puritanical view of spirituality and shame to the subaltern even as they shared resources and hope. Everywhere we have trod has brought a double-edged sword, bringing progress and advances on the one hand, and destroying families, communities and countries on the other.

As Western women, we have pulled ourselves up so far already. We have won the right to vote. We have created a right to childcare in our workplaces, and to equal pay. For the first time in centuries, we have regained choice over pregnancy and the numbers of children we birth. And now, we are looking to the heart, the inner landscape, to address social issues beyond our gender.

Because of our relative privilege in economic and cultural freedoms, we are now the ones who may, if we choose, bring our biology and our hearts together to the front of our global conversation. A conversation which includes the perspectives and needs of our sisters around the world. A conversation surrounding climate, housing, education, human rights and beauty – not just for our own benefit. For the time is ripe, and we are ready, to address our concerns toward unified solutions. We are ready, many of us, to focus our efforts on listening with care, that we might support and nurture resilience that is locally sound. Resilience that acknowledges the unique intricacies and possibilities for every woman's community. In the face of globalisation, and the patriarchal urge it stems from, we as Western women are able to lead redress. Redress that can be more than a band-aid. Redress that at its core empowers.

Others' suffering is something we can address. And the bringing together of diverse views is something we can do. Lifting each other up as sisters, mothers, daughters, we may create a circle of women that interweaves our stories beyond boundaries of nation, race, privilege and location. We may inspire and support each other with due diligence and care.

Voice of the Womb

As an embryo, we were a growing life within the uterus, or womb, of our mother. As an egg, we were within the body of our mother while she was an embryo growing in the uterus of her mother. Every emotion, every feeling, every word spoken and every breath taken by our mother is imprinted upon us. Just as every emotion, every feeling, every word spoken and every breath taken by our grandmother is imprinted within us. For we were present in our grandmother's body as the body of our mother was formed. And we were present in our mother's body while waiting to be formed. We were present in the body of our mother through the whole of her life. And that eventually led to our implantation and growth within her sacred belly. By extending this idea to its natural limits, we find that the memory, emotion and experience of five generations is alive within us. This is true whether we are born male or female. For each one of us came through a womb, and the stories which physically formed our cells are wanting to be heard. What does your womb say, sisters? What do your mothers' wombs say, all humans? This is a voice from my womb, in the early days of the pandemic:

I am weeping today, for those whose lives are passing. For those whose lives are passing from this earthly realm and for those whose lives are passing each day in fear, loneliness or pain. There is so much beauty. This life is more beautiful than we can possibly behold in the short span we have to walk this planet. Infinite realms of colour, sound and majesty are at our fingertips. We have only to open our hearts to see them, feel them, let them in.

For me, this period of the lockdown has been a time of deep transformation and letting go. It has been this for so many. And to each of you, I speak. I feel you, I cry with you and laugh with you and celebrate this magnificent moment on Earth with you. For it is the letting go of 50,000 years of spoilt seeds. It is the letting go of 50,000 years of the subjugation of the feminine. And in the silence and the quiet, my womb has been re-membering and releasing. It is both men and women who have suffered in this last period. The one who harms is in as much pain as the one who is harmed. Of course, there has also been much love, joy and splendid beauty during this period too. As a woman, I cry simply because my body is moving through it. And I allow my body to do so, without attachment and with compassion. I cuddle close to forgiveness and grace. My womb is releasing all the rape, shame, blame, torture, warfare, greed, hoarding and other energies that are not love. And it hurts a little bit as it moves through. It physically hurts. We are the great purifiers, you know. And each month as we bleed, we pass those energies that are not pure love and creation through our very bodies. In this moment in time, the energies coming forth to release are in great rivers and waves. And we are feeling it. Men, we are feeling it. As a womb-man within womb-mankind, my womb is weeping. At the same time though, my heart is expanding.

My heart is expanding inside to new dimensions and new realms I have never imagined. Even with all the spiritual practice I have done, with all the years of intense ecstasy and divine union, there are still ribbons of love unfurling, doorways opening to places of incredible beauty. Places of such immense hope, compassion and equality. And through this, I see the feminine becoming whole. After all these years of feminisms, after all these years of fighting for freedoms, after all these years of waking up to the reality that we are one living breathing human heart, after all of this, the fruit is coming forth. And it comes forth within us and through our bodies.

I feel a great compassion, expansion and equality being born. The power of the human heart to choose love is what I feel awakening in my womb. It is a soft power. It does not fight, it does not protest, it does not blame, *it does not hide. This soft power of the heart simply chooses to love. To love herself. And in that choice, to love others. In that choice, a great unwinding happens. A great unfolding. The release of thousands of years of pain. So I cry right now. And I love, right now. And I see that my feeling is moving me toward hope.* (March 2021)

The Womb of the Earth

From a Sufi perspective the Earth is a jewel among the entire created universes, for she is the womb through which all created life must one day move. Thousands of souls are waiting to incarnate at every moment in order to live the earthly journey through which love is embodied. It is here on Earth that love becomes alive. And it is through the blessing of this Earth that we are given a life which fruits love. In the *Mathnavi*, one of Rumi's many works, it states, 'The angels are patiently watching to see in what condition each human soul will be born'. For it is from Earth that every light being, angel and bodhisattva of the universe first comes. She is the womb of the multiverses. And she has agreed to play this part. It is her great love and sacrifice and joy to create the temples for our souls. Our bodies are not our own, but are borrowed from the soil and stardust and water of the Earth, who is herself a cognisant and conscious being. Her oceans are the amniotic fluid of love itself.

Because of her vital importance and beauty, every soul wishes for an opportunity to be here. Here light, water, soil, gravity and air combine to create the perfect conditions for a unification of spirit and matter. And as women, we are the extensions of her life-giving choice. We are held in her sacred trust. We embody her sacred contract with existence. And it is through our wombs that Earth becomes a space where the heart of love may move through physical form. In slow motion, known as time, the soul may play out its necessary lessons so that it may eventually find freedom and choose love, and then move beyond this plane. And the closer each soul moves to their moment of choice, more and more beauty comes into form. For it is through the human heart that the universal ideal of beauty is birthed. And because of the heart of love, alive within us, that the Earth herself is whole, fruitful and joyous.

From a Sufi perspective, I honour every woman who is now bringing life onto the planet. The souls incarnating at this moment are seeds of a new and bright future. They are arriving with an imprint designed to thrive within that future, and they bring much light and hope for the coming age. The women who are growing their bodies and who will nurture and nourish their hearts and souls – you are providing a road for the continued manifestation of beauty and love for the entire ecosystem of life. And thanks to your sacrifice and devotion, the whole of the created multiverses may benefit.

Voice of the Earth
The Earth is crying,
The Earth has had enough of these tears
And she's asked the sky for his blessings.

The Earth is crying,
The Earth has had enough of these tears
And she's asked the sky for his blessings.

And I do not need to cry anymore,
The Earth can cry for me.

I do not need to cry anymore,
The Earth can cry for me.

For there are much better things I can do with my time,
Like laughing or joking or singing a tune.
I have cried enough tears over you.
Song for the Monsoon[4]

As time moves by, and we move collectively into this long-awaited, long-prophesied, transition we are living, the Earth will want to be heard. Her voice is crucial at this point, and it may surprise us what she has to say. For her voice will come most strongly from the wombs and hearts of the feminine. Climate specialists, scientists, government bodies and agencies may speak on behalf of the Earth. The voice of the Earth is embodied, however, and embodied in the bodies of women. It is women who are in the best position to bring a bright light to the Earth's present dilemmas.

For example, in an estate not five minutes' drive from my home, a group of women organised fruits and vegetables for the local population during our period of lockdown. The estate covers several large hills, some low-lying areas, has a few parks, corners shops and pubs. During our first waves of lockdown, many people in this particular estate had been made redundant or put on furlough at partial capacity of their pay. This made living challenging, and for

---

4 This song is inspired from an original by Claire Louise Hall.

most families all expenditure had to slow, including the weekly food budget. So a couple of women came together, spoke, shared and sparked ideas from the care and compassion of their hearts. They went to as many farmers as possible within the local area and asked to create a scheme for their estate. Within weeks, the wrong size, misshapen, bruised and slightly discoloured fruits and vegetables were no longer going to waste, but were being packaged into food boxes by this group of women. Once a week each family on the large estate received a box with enough fruit and vegetables to more than feed them, and it cost them only £5 if they were earning and £2.50 if they were not. This, dear reader, is the voice of the womb in action, the feminine voice which understands that is has children to feed, that it bleeds.

Women are the light and fuel of culture. Because children are tied to the mother through the nursing years, it is through the mother that children learn to sing, to dance, to notice stars and flowers, to speak kindly. This education, so important to the future of the human as a human, begins from the moment of conception. It begins in the womb. And it is the voice of the mother that is the first imprint on the human, it is her heart that is the first sound, it is her emotion that is the first wave of feeling the child perceives. For this reason, the sensitivities of women have been honoured throughout time. I personally do not buy into ideas of cave dwelling, barbaric humans who did not know how people were formed, how they got into the womb. There are many cosmologies other than the current Western mindset, and most of them place not only women at the centre of the universe, but the human heart as well[5].

The feminine is ripe, right now, to be embodied by an entire species. The peace we are able to generate – as a culture that honours both the female and the feminine – has the potential to be a lasting peace. A peace which may span generations. We have an opportunity in this moment to create release from the oppressions of our past. We may not agree on every issue, for we are as diverse in our embodiments and beliefs as we are unified in our bodies and our hearts. But we can agree that clean air, clean water, and life are sacred. And that we, as one humanity, are the primary protectors and generators of this sacredness.

Women, we cross the threshold of death and life each time we give birth. We are truly fearless in our willingness to honour and bring forth the life within

---

5 For example, the Vedic scriptures tell of the moment when souls descended from the heavens into bodies on Earth. The dwelling of the cosmic soul within the human form was the moment of creation for our species, but not for all of life. The trajectory of animal evolution on the planet was different, and humans entered fully conscious. Sufi and Zoroastrian cosmologies are similar.

us. Let us focus this passion to inspire. And those who are not physically birth-ing, be inspired! For these feminine qualities may be rooted in our biology, but they are waiting to be shared and embodied by all. We are all divine.

The Children's Fire

The Children's Fire

It is early morning. The sun is just peeking over the horizon. Tall grasses catch the sunlight. Dew rests upon the stems and blades. As the Sun warms the earth a light mist rises. Hues of pink and peach stretch across the sky. In the tipis, smoke is rising as the morning fires are being lit. The people are winding their way back from the river nearby, where they have just had their daily bath. Soon they will gather in the morning sun, or if it is raining, under the roof of a long house, and they will share their dreams. Each individual who has had a dream of importance or personal significance in the night will speak, and the community will listen. As the plans for the day are made, they will include new information from the dreams. This is just one of the ways that the Iroquois of the North American Great Lakes region gather and govern themselves.

Across North America there are as many as 600 different tribes or nations, 547 of them federally recognised by the United States government. When we consider that the borders of contemporary nations are not necessarily the borders of related tribes and trade, we can extend this number greatly. And then considering that there are many tribes now long forgotten, we might recognise the existence of thousands of independent indigenous cultures on this land. Language families connect many of the tribes to each other, with dialects differentiating them, as well as customs. The Iroquois Confederacy was made up of the Seneca, Oneida, Onondaga, Cayuga and Mohawk nations (the Five Nations). Later the Tuscarora were added and the confederacy became known as the League of Six Nations. The people's own name for their governing structure is the Haudenosaunee. Many historians date the creation of the Haudenosaunee to the 16th century; however other records place its beginning in the early 12th century. The confederacy was sophisticated, with elected members of each nation forming an overall council. The council, made up of 50 elders, met regularly at the Wampum, or central sacred fire, to make decisions. A full constitution was created that governed all political and legal aspects of a united league of nations, as well as ensuring care and respect for the home, clans and religious ceremonies.

Of particular interest to contemporary conversations on peace and governance is the concept of the peacemaker's fire, created and nurtured by the Iroquois Confederacy. Peacemaker's fire is known in some contexts as the children's fire, which in this naming refers to an important and foundational aspect of the central sacred fire. The central sacred fire was kept in the Onondaga territory, at the centre of the Five Nations area. The elders gathered at this fire several times a year. And as the elders would gather and debate around the fire, every decision would be weighed against its impact on future generations. And that impact was measured not by a vague sense of the future but by the ponderosity of seven future generations. That is a minimum of 150 years – in the indigenous way of counting generations however, this represents 700 years. Let us ask ourselves: How long does it take a tree to mature? How will the water flow be changed, and the water cycles be affected? What will the long-term impact of migration and additional birth have on the land and game? What will the generations coming be interested in, and how will our stories and mythologies continue to speak to them? What are the long-term gains and risks of certain alliances? How might the outcome of any particular war or provision play itself out for our great, great, great, great, great grandchildren? And this way of thinking, of measuring, was considered just the minimum.

In the present moment it is hard to imagine seven generations ahead. Our species and our planet are in a state of transition, and it would behove us to consider our emerging solutions in terms of their long-term impact. Not just for our own lives and those of our children, but for seven generations at a minimum. If we think back seven generations previous to this one, only 20 per cent of people lived in towns, but the migration of huge numbers of people from country to city was on the horizon. The Industrial Revolution, with all of its glamour and pollution alike, was just about to begin. The first vaccinations were given, for smallpox, and the first electric batteries were created. Whole new ways of life, transport and thought were emerging, and these have had an immense impact on the way we live now. If our ancestors and elders had carefully thought through the consequences of each of these huge changes, in light of seven generations, what adjustments and shifts of direction might have been constructed to manage them? What changes would we have chosen not to make? What other possibilities might have emerged, leading to a more abundant, peaceful moment for us now? The concept of the children's fire, as a sacred presence in the very centre of all decision-making, is a concept that can help us. For within this concept, it is not just impact that is considered, but wellbeing, health, abundance and prosperity. Will the children of the future have stories and rituals that keep them balanced, will they know and feel love, and will they too have the presence of mind and heart to continue thinking seven generations beyond themselves?

As we look to the past to inform the present moment, it is important not to romanticise an indigenous past. There is much wisdom, heritage, some phenomenal healing traditions, and incredible ceremonies that we can learn from and admire. There are ways of thinking and being that may help us to remember our connection to the Earth and to each other. And there was also warfare, torture, slavery and cannibalism. Many of the ways of governance and of ceremony were created by the people in order to deal with the very real aspects of human nature that cause us to war. Many of them were designed to deal with the wild and sometimes harsh forces of nature as they are, so that life remained abundant and resources were well managed. As we move more fully into this current time of transition, a clear view of who we are as humans, and what we are capable of, will help us to appreciate a need for sacred structures that help us to create lives of harmony and abundance.

In this chapter I share stories and teachings from the indigenous peoples of North America. In the oral traditions, it is incumbent upon the storyteller to enter into the story fully, through their dreams, their rituals and songs. The way that the story comes through each telling should be fresh, imbued with the insights the teller has brought back from the subtle realms.

The Killing Stops Here

Film is an incredible medium. It brings us into closeness with the characters' inner and outer worlds and allows us to bridge those plains through our own lives and imaginations. There is a film scene that once seen, I have never been able to forget, and because it is relevant I bring it in here.

The wild and white tundra stretches out before the tired warrior Atanarjuat. He has walked days and nights, through moon and stars and snow. He is cold, yet his heart is burning. It is burning for justice and for love. The hills of the distance glow purple in the low setting sun. Midnight blues begin to cover the sky and brilliant stars peek out of the heavens. Seeing smoke from a cooking fire, the warrior knows he is near his destination. Coming close, but not close enough to be noticed, he begins to slice large pieces of ice out of the frozen earth. Stacking them up, he builds a small igloo. As he finishes, he stands tall in the breeze, welcoming the movement of air against his skin, drawing strength from the night. And he waits. As dawn approaches, he moves with the first light, over to the fire he has seen the night before. He approaches the igloo of his companions and calls to them, asking them to come out and meet him. They emerge. They question him. They are surprised to see him. They are caught. And they follow him to the smaller igloo he has built in the night. He enters and they follow. The warrior enters and his companions follow. And standing there, Atanarjuat throws his axe into the centre of the floor between them. He throws his axe down and he says, 'The killing stops here' (Kunuk , 2001). He drew his line in the sand. He drew his line in the ice. And he said, 'The killing stops here'. Where do you draw your line, dear reader? And how do you draw it?

Peacemaker

Peacemaker, as he came to be called, is the Onondaga chief who initiated a call for peace and the forming of the Iroquois Confederacy. He has a name, but the people prefer us not to use it in writing or beyond its sacred utterance. According to tradition, Peacemaker was born of a virgin birth. His mother and grandmother, amidst the warring of their clans' people, had moved north, deep into the forest, to create a life of purity and peace for themselves. The Sky Gods, through the body of the daughter, sent Peacemaker to help the people in this time. When he came of age, the mother and daughter went back to the people and Peacemaker began his mission (Moss). In other tellings it is said that Peacemaker was born of one tribe and raised by another. Some say he was born a Huron and raised by the Onondaga, others that he was born Ononda- ga and raised by the Mohawk. In any case, such a scenario would have been common in that time, due to the intertribal warfare and the taking of slaves. Both scenarios are probably true. From the strife of the people, from the expe- rience of Peacemaker's heart, from his dreams and relations with the Sky Gods, a deep prayer for peace was born within him. And as he matured that prayer became clear. Peacemaker saw, or was given, the methods for cleansing the minds of the people and for establishing a lasting peace between them. And as the time came for Peacemaker to begin sharing those visions, he realised he would need some helpers.

One of Peacemaker's helpers was Hiawatha, a man who had fallen so far from grace that he had forgotten he even had a family. He was living in the forest in the most slovenly of conditions when Peacemaker came to him. Peacemaker cleansed him and healed him, and Hiawatha became his spokes- person. Together Peacemaker and Hiawatha travelled across the Five Nations territories. Convincing warriors and chiefs, who were deep into their craft, to embrace peace was not an easy mission. But together they brought the energies of peace, and through them the people began to see the goodness of a new way. Peacemaker and Hiawatha held the vision, and little by little the warriors and the chiefs began to choose to lay down their weapons.

And as that sharing was received, a new culture and a new structure for life began to emerge. The confederacy that Peacemaker dreamed, which led the people into several hundred years of peace, began to take shape. The central symbol of that structure became a pine tree. A tall white pine, with an eagle nesting in the top, under which the elders of all five tribes of the Iroquois confederacy buried their weapons. A tall white pine under whose branches those first elders of peace spoke. A tall white pine under which they made the first agreements. Agreements to uphold the peace of the household, to protect each other, to lay down their weapons and to value equality as a unifying principle. A sacred fire was lit, at the centre, near the pine tree, and it was agreed to keep this sacred fire burning. Custodians of the fire were called upon. And the fire became known as the Peacemaker's fire. Through the land the elders moved, speaking in turn to their own people. Through the land the ideals of peace, nonviolence, equality and the protection of children were taken up. Through the land sacred fires were lit and prayers were said. Through the hearts of the people a structure for peace was born. And this peace lasted many generations and went forth into the world. And this peace, it keeps the happiness and health of the next seven generations at its centre. The children's fire still burns today. There are specific ways for lighting and sharing it. The fire is carried from one sacred location to another by the sacred fire keepers, and today it burns on almost every continent. And here, I would like to tell the story of another peacemaker.

Another Peacemaker

This story is not unrelated to the first. In some tellings, the woman is known as New Face, and she is part of Iroquois mythology and legend. In my own journeys with her, she lives in the desert, among the tribes of the Southwest.

Among the tribes of the Southwest, there was a beautiful young lady, more beautiful than you can imagine. She had thick, long, black hair that fell in large curls down her back. She was round and soft yet incredibly strong in her body. She was smart too. But most importantly, her heart and her eyes were shining. As she grew, she became aware of the attention she drew. And as her awareness woke up in this way, she became aware of the power it wielded. She began to use this power to her advantage, and to take men into her life and her bed in exchange for the acclaim and riches they could offer. As the time went by, her home became larger and more ornamented. Her clothes became finer and softer, with more decoration and colour. Her possessions grew in number and value. But her heart began to weaken, her eyes began to lose their shine. She found herself again and again waking up with a silent longing in her soul. As the time went by, she could no longer fool herself that she was hurting. It was easy to keep up appearances. It was easy to keep the men coming. But inside, a great transformation was beginning. Great Spirit was calling her, and then came the day she could no longer ignore it.

Awaking early one morning, just as the grey light of dawn was stretching itself across the low horizon, the girl awoke in a fit of internal agony. She threw herself out of bed and looked across the desert. Her eyes saw a jackrabbit running, the early morning flowers open to gather the dew and the last of the stars fading into light. She felt as grey inside as the pre-dawn. Nothing inspired her. Until she saw the crescent Moon. The tiniest sliver, just barely enough to glimpse. The girl beheld the Moon and in that moment she made a decision. A decision that would change the rest of her life. And following on that decision, she put on her boots and drew up her leggings. Put a coat over her dress. And she walked out into the desert. She walked out with no food and no water and not much hope either. And she walked. She had no direction in mind. And she didn't know if she was coming back. She only knew that she was following an urge within her heart that had been long ignored. So she walked through the morning, until the Moon rose and disappeared from the growing light of the Sun's rays. Until the jackrabbit and jackdaw hid from sight under the shelter of distant rocks. Until the dew had left the earth and evaporated from the air. Until she was parched, sweaty and exhausted. She was nearly ready to die, and having no direction, she simply lay down on the desert floor and surrendered. She surrendered all of herself. To death, to life, to the will of the desert and the will of her soul. After a long time, baked, browned, burnt and throbbing, she finally began to cry. From where the tears came, in that parched body of hers, she did not know. But they felt good and they tasted good and for many hours they cleansed her soul. Finally, the girl fell asleep.

When she awoke it was late in the night. The Moon had disappeared from the sky. The air was cold, dew just beginning to form. Nothing stirred. Even the coyote was asleep. And in this space, this endless place of pure air and relentless sky and horizon, the girl's heart awoke. In the midst of total darkness, the girl's heart awoke. And as it awoke it hurt. Oh, did it hurt. And it ached.

And her whole body began to ache. And she moaned into the night. A moan of longing for her creator, for that being and that love and that power that is more than her. And that beingness, that love, that power, it came. It came in the form of a luminous white light in the midst of all that dark sky. And the white light surrounded her, entered her, enfolded her, and healed her soul. That light, it made her sing. A song of rasping voice and keening, but a song nonetheless. And that light, it made her sit up and look across the desert. And in that moment the girl claimed her life back, she claimed her heart. And as she stood, she saw that the light came from within her. And she knew it was good.

Walking back to her home, she lifted her chin, she lifted her eyes, and her heart began to beat within her stronger. Arriving home, the girl shut and locked the front door. Some say she saw no visitors for days, some say weeks, others insist it was months. What we do know is the girl spent time alone. She tidied her space. She removed the things that made her feel heavy. She filled the space with light. She opened her throat and began to sing. And in time, her eyes began to shine again. When the girl felt ready, she opened her front door to the world once more. But this time she put two rocking chairs on the porch. And a table with a pitcher of endless lemonade. And a feeder for the birds. And the girl began to welcome the men as they approached her home once again. Only this time she did not take them inside. Instead, she taught them of a different kind of beauty. The beauty of the light within her. Her own light. Her sacred wellspring of wellbeing. And she talked for many long hours with the men. And she told them of the way of knowing peace. And she told them of the story of the Moon. Of the way she heard Great Spirit calling. And she inspired many men to seek out the voice of Great Spirit. And she inspired many women to walk into the desert and seek their inner knowing, their inner beauty. And in time, her reputation grew. Mothers would send their daughters to learn from her. And men would come from far and wide, for the healing conversation and presence of her being. And in time, she became known as a peacemaker. For she brought peace to many.

White Buffalo Calf Woman

Moving to the Lakota peoples, of the Northern Great Plains, where the modern-day Dakotas, Montana, Wyoming and parts of Canada stretch – we encounter the story of White Buffalo Calf Woman. She is a goddess and her rituals for peace are a regular and enduring part of the Lakota peoples. This is one of her stories.

The people were warring between themselves. It had been escalating for some time, and the elders were carrying much concern. The elders, they made prayers. And by and by, three warriors had an encounter in the fields. They were out, walking and talking, scouting and surveying the land, generally talking with each other in a relaxed way, and in the distance they saw an apparition. A light. The light was nearly 20 feet tall and just as wide, and in the centre of that light was a woman. A beautiful woman. And they knew, the warriors knew, this must be a goddess. They were afraid. But being the ones to witness the vision, they knew they must approach her. Eventually, one of them stepped forward, said he would go. He walked toward the goddess and as he came closer he saw that her beauty was formidable. Her presence washed over him and he trembled. Bowing on one knee he said, 'I bow before you goddess, what is it you wish to impart to me?'.

The man bowed on one knee and the goddess began to speak. White Buffalo Calf Woman began to speak. And she spoke of love, of care, and of an end to the time of war. The people had called and she had come. She gave to the young warrior seven rites, or rituals, which would, when kept regularly, keep the peace. These rituals included purification through bathing, or the sweat lodge. Healthy and inclusive communication rites, through the passing of the peace pipe. She shared the Sun Dance, for the initiation of men. And rites for women when they begin puberty. The goddess shared rituals for the naming of boys and the naming of girls, and rituals for the passage at death. She shared every detail, and the warrior absorbed it all. Finally, she revealed her prophecy. And this prophecy states that the people are to keep the rites faithfully, and when an all-white buffalo calf is born, they will know that finally peace is dawning for all humankind. For the goddess was part woman, part white buffalo. Half woman, half white buffalo. And the power of the buffalo was within her, and she was surrounded by white light.

The warrior gave great thanks to the goddess, and trembling with a mixture of joy, fear and anticipation, he rose. He promised to impart the vision in every detail, and began to walk back to his friends. Reaching them, he stood with the power of the goddess coursing through him and related all. And the friends, witnessing the sacredness of the moment, bowed their heads. Then, giving each other a big grin and a pat on the back, the boys returned to the tribe. Relating all that they had seen and experienced, the rites and rituals were soon integrated by the Lakota. The elders smiled and gave thanks. And in 1984 'the first' all-white buffalo calf was born in the area of Wisconsin.

These stories have a common theme, a common thread. And that thread, as much as it is the bringing of peace, speaks to how peace arises within humanity. These stories begin with a time of conflict, either inner or outer. They begin at the moment the suffering is too much to bear. For it is in such moments that we as humans become ready to listen. We bow, we lay down our bodies, we lay down our weapons. We surrender to that which is greater than ourselves. And through this surrender, born of the heart, a vision is given, an impulse is followed, a visitation is made from Great Spirit/the universe/divine love. And like all heros' or heroines' journeys, the individual goes back to the tribe with a teaching, a gift. And then the real work comes. The rites of purification to follow, the setting up of structures, the sharing of our gift. And it is from the living of the gift, from the sharing of it in the daily walk, that peace becomes manifest between us.

A Big Choice

Chief Arvol Looking Horse, an elder of the Lakota people, is the current carrier of the White Buffalo Calf medicine bundle. He speaks to our current transitions,

> *There are many nations upon the earth, but we all have our spiritual foundation. After the white buffalo calf was born – when we journeyed back, that was the first time that I made a statement, that we are at the crossroads. We are going to be faced with a lot of chaos, disasters. We are going to see a lot of tears, not just from our relatives' eyes. We are going to see global changes, earthquakes, volcanoes where it never happened before. We are going to see a lot of sicknesses and viruses. We are going to see a lot of anger, hatred. We are going to see a lot about false prophets and false leaders. We live in a time when man, human beings, have lost repute. No more honourable words, it's going to be all about money. We are at the crossroads, where we can unite spiritually, globally, like today, world peace and prayer day, uniting all nations, all faiths, one prayer. And that statement in 1996 is still... today we are in those times right now. (2021)*

Between 1996 and the present moment, Chief Looking Horse has spoken and prayed with many people. His messages of unity and responsibility help focus the love we have for each other towards grounded solutions:

What's happening in the world today, with global warming, we can't – me or a group of people, a handful of people – we can't really… it's got to be global. That's why we talk about global warming, it's got to be a spiritual unity in the world today. These prophecies are there, the white buffalo, the white animals, the eagle and the condor, there's so many prophecies, even in the Bible, there are different people that talk about different things in these prophecies during this time right now. But it's going to take all people to really come together, with the heart, with the heart and the mind. Because in the past it's seemed like, my way is the only way. For me, I can't say that I want everybody to pick up a (sacred) pipe, I'm not here to speak about that. I'm pushing that responsibility to the people, the people in general. Because we all love our kids and we all have the gift of compassion, responsibility. People's responsibility – in order for this earth to survive there's got to be peace and harmony, there's that balance that we have to create. This is my message, that we are going to create this. (2010)

Remembering the painting on the red rock face, we may choose, as we are beings of free will, to allow ourselves to step up along the staircase of phenomenal intelligence, to expand our knowing into new heart-based perceptions – or – we may choose to walk as we are, living the natural consequences and outcomes of life within this choice. Life which includes sickness, war, slavery, and harm.

Another elder, from the Hopi Nation, describes further indications of our moment of choice:

It is said that human will not know if they are man or woman, that people will forget the body is a sacred portal – seeing it merely as flesh and bones, and that women will wear war paint to make themselves beautiful[1] (Banyacya, 1995).

---

1 Women of the East have long used kohl and pigments to beautify themselves, as well as henna. They have excelled in the braiding and keeping of their hair, and ornamentation through jewellery is part of the ancient ways the world over. The difference is not if humans make themselves beautiful, but how we use these tools. We might consider our use of plastics in our skin and our need to wear makeup just to leave the house as acts similar to those of a warrior putting on paint to face the darkness. The natural beauty of a woman and a human shines through when we are purified in love, with or without paint and ornamentation.

To me, these indications speak to our distortion and subjugation of the feminine principle, which we have discussed in previous chapters. For now, let us say that the feminine principle is intrinsically tied to peace. For peace to flower, energies of care, truth and our inborn creative power must become central to our thought, feeling and action.

Sexual Energies and Purification

Our sexual energies are some of the most potent vibrations in existence[2]. They are the life force of the planet moving upward through us, in the same way the life force moves through a plant and causes it to push out of the ground and reach upward. Ideally, these energies are cultivated and refined, so that as they rise, they move through the will power centre of the solar plexus and then through the heart. Combusting in the heart with the visionary fire of the upper chakras, the life force of the planet becomes unified with the energy of the Sun. The power of this union is a heavenly fire, the fire of love in all of its most beautiful and refined forms, and the power of creation. Because this unified energy is so powerful, it has of course been appropriated and misused. There are all sorts of ways the life force of the planet, as it moves through us as sexual energy, gets weighed down and distorted. Obvious ways are institutions such as pornography and sex trafficking, but equally heavy and subversive are energies of shame, blame, judgement and fear. Because the sexual energies move in an upward fashion, from earth and water into fire and love, they can get stuck in muck and mud. That muck is often formed of unprocessed emotion. Grief, rage, loss – these all distort the life force.

There was a time when we understood as human beings the movement and nature of our energies. This includes the vital energy of our sexual centres, the fire of our willpower, our capacity for love, our sacred breath and our connection to the dreamtime. We understood the value of metabolising grief through fire for instance. We understood that a hard day's work spent and regenerated the life force in a positive way. We understood that softly singing to ourselves in times of loneliness and loss was in fact the medicine and the cure. Time for feeling, for laying on the Earth and being held by her, for being 'in' the

---

2 In the story of Peacemaker, earlier in this chapter, there is a sorcerer who casts psychic darkness, pestilence and pain over the people. He does so through the use of his enormous, venomous penis-snake. The sexual energies, misused, have an incredible power to harm. Part of Peacemaker's work is to defeat the sorcerer, and he does so by confronting and cleansing him. The sorcerer, once cleansed, becomes a powerful part of the peacemaking confederacy.

Sun and receiving his warmth, for witnessing each other, and for the arts was non-negotiable. Life was integrated in this way, where science and spirituality, work and love, family and community were intertwined. And this was natural, because it helped us to survive and thrive. And this was part of how we, as a species, purified ourselves continually.

If we remember the teachings and ritual gifts of White Buffalo Calf Woman, we see that they each address aspects of how the life force moves within us. Purification is important at all levels, physical, emotional, mental and spiritual. Purification happens through connection with the Earth, with spirit and with each other. If we think back on Peacemaker and his message of peace, it is through purification of the will power, through the laying down of arms, through clear communication and commitments, that the muck and mud that carry distortion are released. If we look back at the beautiful story of Peacemaker the woman, we see that tears, the Moon, surrender and grace lead to purification. Hers is a story of metabolising emotion so that the sexual life force may flow like a pure glistening spring. This is a story of the willpower to use the sacred breath for teaching. This is a story of surrender of the personal will and drive for gratification to the larger life force, that of divine love, expressed in us as union.

If we are to dream in a new world so that it is full of abundance, prosperity, health, music, laughter, beauty and love – then we must necessarily attend to purification. Is this aspect of our evolution not a central part of the collective choice we are making?

Time and Manifestation

We have spoken about the movement of epochs across time. Consciousness has evolved through four worlds already, and we are in the process now of moving into a fifth. Each of these worlds has had its own wave of cycles within it, periods of peace and clear knowing alternating with periods of darkness and forgetting. As we move yet again through a major portal, memories of our earlier movements may return to us[3]. The veil of time separating past, present and future is thin in moments of transition. It is even possible we might see glimpses of future eras and later transitions, as our elders before us have.

---

3 For example, the golden ages of Lemuria are well known in the Vedic oral tradition. The aboriginal peoples of Australia have in their oral tradition the golden age of Earth's dawn. Many people these days have memories of Egypt, though that particular age was full of troubles of its own.

In Sufism there is a concept called jumping out of time. This relates both to the moment of death, and to movements across dimensions. Through trance, the Sufi moves fluidly between the present moment and its dense, vibrational realities – to the subtle or spiritual planes, where time is more thin and causality and manifestation take more fluid roles with each other. This is related to quantum physics, which describes how a dot or point of existence pulsates and waves of vibration and creation move out from it. That point is a point outside of time. We move through it at death – where it is often described as a tunnel that opens into a light. We also have the capacity to move through this point into many worlds, while still alive in this one, through the medium of trance. In this way Sufis are said to taste death before they die. In the Iroquois tradition, dreaming is a way to move through death many times prior to the death of our physical form. Such mysteries are a part of the teachings of many spiritual systems, including both religions and older, shamanic ontologies.

There exists within our species a capacity to jump outside of time – in the North American indigenous people's language this is called entering the Sky World. We carry this collectively and it is a part of our blood and bone memory. The particles of water circulating on the planet carry the memory of our previous movements. And because we are in a moment of transition between worlds, it is possible right now to move through visionary and subtle dimensions spontaneously.

Over the last two years I have had clients regularly coming to me with visitations and visions from other dimensions and other worlds. Some are experiencing the physical sensations that accompany the awakening of their energy bodies. This is partly due to the rhythm of the Earth's movement within our galaxy and the accumulation of speed through precession. Our current position creates a faster rotation and therefore sense of time[4]. According to some scholars, time has been speeding up for millions if not billions of years, little by little, through the precession of the equinoxes (Clow, 2007). Because of precession, the Earth is always in a new relationship to both our own Sun and the outer cosmos. We are physically never in the same place twice, and in our current relationship, we are spinning faster than ever before. Some would say that it is because of our current planetary position within the galaxy that we are moving into a fifth world. That the cycles of our geological and galac-

---

4 Precession has been understood by the ancients across cultures. In the Vedic scriptures it is explained in great detail according to mathematical application. At its basis there are ascending and descending undulations which move in 12,000 year arcs, thus forming our ages of remembering and forgetfulness (Yogananda, p. 187).

tic rhythms are in effect working on us to remember our true potential and consider how we will move forward. I bring the aspect of precision into the conversation here to affirm that we are part of a rhythmical, known pattern. It is partly because we are at a particular juncture in the pattern that we have the opportunity to transition in a big way. This is in part why the white buffalo calf was born to us now. Our stories, prophecies and physical reality come together to help us make sense and make good choices.

As time speeds up, manifestation becomes quicker. Through a natural, rhythmical opening of the spiritual and subtle planes to our awarenesses, we may slowly become cognisant of our capacity as creators. And if anger, grief, loss, shame and pain are unmetabolised within us, they will sprout and quickly grow roots. To ensure a world of beauty not only for ourselves, but for the next seven generations, purification must be attended to.

Pinyos and the Seeds

Every thought, feeling and action has the potential to create entire forests of existence. In Ecuador, from the indigenous peoples of South America, there is a legend and a story that illustrates the power of the seeds we plant and the choices we make. This legend is part of the Shuar oral tradition, who are themselves part of the larger Quechua family of nations. Because this story illustrates such a powerful concept, and it has played such an important part in my life, I share it with you here.

The Shuar say that for millions and millions of years the people lived peacefully. They lived in family clans, led by the mothers and grandmothers, moving gently on the land. The Earth was wild and the people were part of it. Then one day, something changed. One of the people of the tribe – his name was Pinyos – harmed another. He committed the first harm. And then he watched, as the one who he had harmed, harmed another. And the one who had been harmed, they harmed yet another. As the harm began to spread through his family clan, Pinyos began to feel regret. Then one day, one of the adults who had been harmed, they harmed a child. And the child who had been harmed, well they went and harmed another. And as the harm began to move child to child, destroying the family, Pinyos began to feel not only regret, but deep remorse. 'What have I done!', he thought to himself. And he went into the jungle.

Pinyos went into the jungle and he walked. And he walked. And he walked and he walked and he walked and he walked. He followed the river. He took no food, no water with him, just followed the river and sought out his soul.

And some say he walked for three days, some for three weeks and others say it was three months. Finally, after a long, long journey, Pinyos came to the place where two rivers meet. And there, where the two rivers meet, was a lagoon. The water was an exquisite turquoise blue. Tall reeds and birds of paradise whispered and ruffled at the edges of the water. And at the back was an enormous waterfall, cascading down. In the middle of the lagoon was a being of light, 15 feet tall, radiating brilliance. And the being of light smiled at Pinyos, he called him near. Pinyos, trembling, stepped into the lagoon. He stood there, his soul naked in the being's presence, and the being of light handed him a magical vine. The being told Pinyos how to prepare the vine, how to cultivate it and how to use it. He cleansed and he blessed Pinyos and he breathed the essence of love into his spirit. And Pinyos was overcome with gratitude.

Pinyos knelt at the edge of the lagoon, weeping like a baby. He wept with joy and he wept with relief and he wept with sorrow to cleanse his anger and his shame. And when he was done weeping, he rose to his feet. Pinyos stood tall and he rose to his feet. He bathed in the waterfall and he sang a song of thanksgiving to the being of light. And with a smile shared between them, a deep reciprocity, Pinyos turned and began the long walk back along the river. He walked. And he walked. And he walked and he walked and he walked and he walked. He followed the river. He took no food, no water with him, just followed the river, but this time with a little more purpose, a little more hope. And as Pinyos walked, all the animals of the jungle, the birds and the snakes and the mammals, they all came to the path that Pinyos walked, and they taught him their songs. Chirriup, chirriup. Cooli cooli cooli cooli coo cooli coo cooli coo coo coo. Chereee chereee. Then one morning, as Pinyos crested a mountain ridge, he saw his family village in the distance below. He picked up his pace, clambering down the steep sides as fast as he could go. And when he reached the village, straight away he began to prepare the magical vine. He planted some to cultivate. He gathered some leaves and bound them together. He stirred the cooking pot. And he called the children to him. Pinyos gave the children the magical preparation. And he sat them down, and with the bundle of leaves, he began to sing over them the songs of the birds, the animals, the forest. One by one he removed the seeds of harm. And the Shuar say that we will just keep doing this until all the seeds of harm are gone.

What a beautiful story! Due to the fast nature of manifestation in the now, it is important that the seeds we plant are whole, fully imagined, pure and with heart intention. As creators, the power of our focus cannot be understated. Emotion is powerful, and can create either beauty or pain, clarity or mud. Intentionality in thought, in speech, in feeling actually determines what or who we feed. In the vast subtle plains, where the eagles fly, even a hair to the right or left results in seeds of distortion. So in this time of rapid manifestation, try to really comprehend the consequence of precision and care in our thought, emotion and speech. With every breath we are planting seeds. They grow forests – forests that our children and children's children will be living with for the next seven generations. If the world we are living in now is the result of seeds planted long ago, this can be an indicator to us of just how much care we need to bring to the present moment. To grow a world of reciprocity and balance, we begin with planting and nurturing seeds of love.

Beauty and the Way of Love

In Sufism there is a balance between the way of knowledge and the way of love. In both the inner world and the outer manifest world, love is the central core. Knowledge may be seen to orbit around love, with love being the nucleus of life. This is because knowledge without love leads to an imbalance. But a knowledge that is saturated with love attends to each moment with true understanding and consideration. As we gather the knowledge of these powerful stories, let's allow them to imprint us, to open us a little further to love.

To learn to see beauty is a skill. Patiently training the mind, the emotions, our words toward beauty, we begin to formulate distilled and purified responses to life. Such responses become a beacon that shines into all dimensions. They act as a healing balm and are pleasant, like a beautiful fragrance. To discipline oneself, to train the mind and emotions toward beauty, is an act of continuous mindfulness. The spiritual masters have for certain walked the beauty way, and we can see in some people an inner light, which is their beauty. Holding it lightly, because it is so important, we learn from beauty the power of our yes and the power of our no. For 'No' is all we ever have to say to any energy other than love. While this is easy to forget, through a lightly held discipline of the moment to moment beingness of ourselves, we begin to still the worry of the mind, and to purify our human nature. From beauty arises a simplicity, which helps us to navigate the considerations of life. A simplicity that is able to hold the rich complexity of those considerations in balance.

These are times of transition, and how long this transition lasts none of us can say. As we fortify our inner worlds in order to last the change, it is especially important that we cultivate surrender to love. For with love comes trust in our hearts and their inner guidance. As we move from the fourth into the fifth world, we can and should bring the beauty we have cultivated with us. It is more important than ever right now that our appreciation of nature be nourished. Our incredible cultures of music, arts, colour and handicrafts can be witnessed, honoured and made resilient through learning them. Likewise, our many diverse languages can be appreciated for the ways they help us to think differently, and with care and consideration brought into our larger global conversations. It is important right now that we laugh, and that we treasure our human connection. Joy can move us out of fear and toward stillness. And from stillness, we make better decisions. Let us think on the intrinsic laughter of children who are safe and loved. Let us receive the aqueduct of richness moving with us across time, the memories of hope and joy and tears that are our silt and soil to plant in. The human is aligned to beauty by nature and our capacities for seeing and creating it are endless. Let's let our gratitude for this aspect of ourselves lead the way. As we act with love and acquire knowledge that serves, we will be amazed with the power of our hearts and their outpourings.

The importance of beauty cannot be underestimated in our current crises. When we focus on beauty we naturally bring our full love into a central point of consideration[5]. Beauty does not tolerate to harm another, even if it is for 'the greater good'. Beauty is not satisfied with incoherence, or with selfishness. Beauty flows like water and naturally seeks harmony. So a much simpler way to focus on bringing harmony and peace to the planet – and her people – is simply to know, reflect and create beauty within and around us. There need not be polarised opposites and divisions, because all peoples are beautiful. And all divisions can be melted in the beauty of the heart. For example, science and spirituality are both beautiful – incredibly beautiful, especially when their main focus is transformation and true health. In creating our solutions, we can move beyond war-imprinted band-aids that can only hope to relieve the virus of the moment. We must necessarily engage our concerns from a holistic lens, and this means that the way of beauty, the way of love, may meet the way of knowledge and the way of reason. In the lagoon where these two rivers meet, we might find ourselves humbled, weeping, with fresh perspectives and new tools to bring forward. For it is at the meeting points of diverse systems where new life emerges. Each is a part, and the whole is bigger than all of the parts.

---

5 There is also a path of beauty in the North American indigenous people's ways. The Navajo of the Southwest have a beautiful story not dissimilar to the Cinderella story, and the girl child brings back the rites and rituals known as the Beauty Way. It is a full path, like White Buffalo Calf Woman's path, and helps the people to remember and cultivate beauty as a collective community.

Right now, doctrinal religion can be brought into the heart and there transformed. Right now, drugs and pharmaceutical science can be brought into the heart and there be transformed. And any structure of rigidity, no matter how much knowledge it adds to the equation, may now be brought into the heart so that a truly useful set of approaches may emerge which sustain life, goodness, beauty and health.

Quality

It was in *Zen and the Art of Motorcycle Maintenance* (Pirsig, 1991) that I first came into the concept of quality. I was a teenager and didn't fully understand what the author was referring to. As I have grown however, I comprehend more each day what quality means. And for me, right now, quality is a way and an approach that induces fluid and resonant response to the moment.

In the religious cosmologies of the East there are many emanations of God. From the one come the many, from the creatrix comes the creator, the father, the mother, the universes and all beings. Likewise in Islam, from the one comes the infinite. The 99 names of Allah, which represent infinity, help us to see that everything we experience is an emanation of the one. And it is up to us what we choose to feed, to live and to speak into being. From a singularity, all qualities arise. And what we choose to focus on, to speak into reality and to live in an embodied form, are the qualities that will pervade our shared realities.

Equally important as pure seeds, for the future of life and the beauty of existence, are the qualities of compassion and non-judgement. In the bigger picture, all of manifestation is simply on its way home to love. Where we perceive any being or situation in its journey is not its final destination. Perhaps a person needs to experience greed in order to let go of greed, for instance. Or perhaps we have needed, as a species, to give up our human connections and freedoms so that we may learn to value and consciously choose them. According to the Sufis, when a seed of love or beauty emerges in the heart of a person, we say that they are free, and it is not up to us if it is in this or any other lifetime. To receive the seed of our freedom, and to do our best – every moment and every day – to nurture it, this is what we can do. We accept and love each person as they are, holding the light of their freedom in our presence – for it is manifested and real whether we live to see it or not. What a person may still need to experience, in order to release into love and freedom fully, is not ours to judge. And the time that it takes for each soul to mature is between that soul and God. It is not our business. Our business is to see beauty in them. For by seeing beauty, the beautiful qualities of manifestation become more embodied.

Our perception is important. In the act of seeing each other in our freedom and light, as beautiful beings, we actually bring these qualities into existence. Our perception, held lightly in the tenderness of our generative heart, reflects that which is beautiful back to a person. In this sense, attainment, enlightenment, or realisation, is not a solitary endeavour. It is by our co-perception that we elevate collectively. This is the fragility and the power of creation in action. This is how we are God-beings, created in God's image, with the ability to create. And of course such a power can be harnessed or used for ulterior motives. We have seen the misuse of our subtle and powerful capacity in every existing government and religion of our recent civilisations. And it is a reclaiming of this power that will allow us as a global population to work together, in cooperation. This is spiritual sovereignty. And as we come together, we will necessarily encounter not only love, but all of the suppressed and hidden qualities which must come to the surface in order to be released.

Desmond Tutu, speaking in the aftermath of the Rwanda Civil War, emphasises that qualities of compassion and forgiveness are not without boundaries. To come together in cooperation, we simply must forgive, because it is the only way to release the energies of harm. When we forgive however, we do not forget. We choose to honour the richness and reality of our diversity while holding the singularity of our love up to the Sun (2013; 2014). In South Africa, Tutu's work in the Truth and Reconciliation Commission was pioneering in that amnesty was offered in exchange for truth. To be truthful, to speak from the heart, in order to release the harm it caused, allows a person to soften and to redefine for themselves clear boundaries, connection and safety[6].

So, what do the qualities of our emerging fifth world feel like and what may be manifested there? The answer is, it is up to us. From our traditions and from nature, we can take some indications as to the possibilities. In Sufism, the number five is the number of love. In Hindu and East Indian cosmologies, the fifth energy centre of the human bio-energy field is blue and the essence of the voice. Blue is the expanse of the sky, and where the energies of the heart rise into a shared collective vision or embrace. As the fourth world is teaching us about sovereignty, compassion and reciprocity, the fifth world can be a place of unity and peace.

---

6 Desmond Tutu played an important role in the moral and spiritual leadership of peoples effected by apartheid in South Africa and civil war in Rwanda. Upon election, Nelson Mandela appointed him to help redress the deep wounding of South African peoples, in both political and spiritual ways.

Summation

We have an opportunity right now to influence the way the fifth world comes into being. The monumental nature of this opportunity has caused many competing agendas to seek out and hold our attention. Each would have us put our emotion, and the power behind that, which is our heart, toward their own purposes. We, however, have a choice. Consciousness did not evolve to this point to suddenly stop. The waves of time will keep moving, and the Earth will keep spinning, and the Sun will keep shining. So we might as well choose to focus our intention, our emotion, our heart power, toward the hope and beauty of the next seven generations. To those who would like to grow forests that provide clean air, water and shelter for the coming generations: we must plant them now. Those who would like to grow forests that provide happiness, freedom and peace: we have the chance to plant them right now. Those who would like to grow forests of pure divine love and presence: we can radiate a light that cleans. And the way to do this planting is the best way you know how. The time for indulging in decisions about who we really want to be is over. You will learn as you go, if you are committed. And this is the essence of purification. Humility and commitment, learning as we go, constantly shedding and growing. Purification is a healthy and continuous bottom line for a world of harmony. A gentle purification, imbued with compassion and love. For each one of us has the opportunity to do as Peacemaker has, as Pinyos has, to follow the river of our heart until we find the remedy, and to bring that back for the next seven generations.

Chapter Five

Our Golden Opportunity

We are at the Nile's end,
We are carrying particles from every continent,
Creature and age.

I only hear these words from God
Where we are all now trying to embrace
The clear sky ocean,

Dear ones, come. Please,
My dear ones come.
Hafiz

A Universal Esoteric Platform

We have come here, to the Nile's end. We have come here from every ocean, across every expanse of time. We have come here to migrate into our next evolutionary consciousness together, unified in Love.

Where oceans meet, they mix and merge. Distinct, yet one, their currents flow both next to and within each other. Sweet and salty, river and sea also meet. Moisture rises from their union and gathers as clouds, falls and tumbles in complete surrender and forms rainbows. So it is with the many traditions and systems of spirituality that have guided us these past 50,000 years. Each one is full of richness, beauty and truth. Each one has guided many souls to the ocean of divine love. And yet each one retains its colours, its specificity. As we bathe in the waters of our own tradition we dance, mix and merge with the waters of others. And thus we embody the principle of unity through diversity.

The Universal Esoteric Platform is a Sufi term that speaks to a time where our world's spiritual traditions encounter each other in openness and truth (Friedlander, 2003). It is a time where the root of divine love is found to be foundational. A deep respect is born among us for all the ways we return to love. Through our movement into cities worldwide, plus many earlier and current migrations, many traditions now live side by side. And as part of this mixing, many of us now embody multiple traditions within the house of our own body and being.

To function in a way of rootedness to our own traditions, with respect and appreciation of others, is a path to unity, grounded in equanimity. Unity is a grounded possibility, one which springs directly from love. A love of self and other which goes far beyond tolerance. For in tolerance, we can still hang onto an idea that we are better somehow, that we are right. Rumi writes,

Through Love, the bitter becomes sweet
Through Love, copper becomes gold
Through Love, dregs becomes clear
Through Love, pains become healing
Through Love, the dead become living
Through Love, the king becomes a slave.
Mevlana Jalaluddin Rumi (Masnavi II:1529-3)

Here, Rumi speaks to love as the essential ingredient in transformation. And it is through the transforming of our prejudices and judgements by which a possibility of love beyond tolerance emerges. In Rumi's time, people gathered around him because of his deep love. His teachings and guidance created a community and from this community the order of Sufism which follows his teachings came into being. In the Mevlevi Order, named after Rumi's title of Mevlana, love is the glue which holds the universe together. Through our process of surrendering to love, we may dance and move together in unity.

Unity is both a grounded and a metaphysical concept. Unity is both an inside job and a job of relations. When true unity is a reality, inner and outer are reflected in one another in perfect harmony. Bitter and sweet, pain and healing, dregs and opalescence, death and birth, they are one in the embrace of love. Coming into one is a merging of the ideas which categorise and separate, a collection of the fragments which live apart, a melting of the resistances which keep the magnetism of all opposites separate. Rumi also writes, 'It is not our task to seek for love, but to seek and remove all the barriers we have put in the way of love'. So inner unity is about crumbling, surrender, to the great force from which our vibration came and comes into being. And outer unity is the movement of that internal state into meeting points with other universes, other selves.

If we desire peace upon this planet, then the first place to find it or create it, is within. And to discover peace within our sovereignty, the very power of our hearts, we must bow to love. To the love from which we came and to which we return.

To get to the source of divine love and union, it is helpful to have a tradition. My encouragement then is to choose a path, and whichever path you choose, follow it to its depths, its hardships and joys, until you reach the source. From our roots and our traditions, with humility and grace, we may share the fruits of our paths with the other oceans we find ourselves next to.

A Time of Power

Many of the elders have spoken, from many nations, all carrying the same truth. When elder Thomas Banyacya (1909–1999) has spoken of the time we are living in now, he has emphasised our moment of choice. Referencing the rock painting of stick figures and a staircase (Chapter 1), Banyacya presents it as the story of an older and a younger brother. The older brother is a Hopi and the younger one the white man. The younger brother may choose to take back his power, to return to sacred ritual and to keeping the sacred rites, or he may not. If he does not, the Earth will destroy the environment again. At this moment in time, however, the younger brother, the one who must make the choice, may wake up (1995).

This is a time of incredible opportunity. And because of this opportunity, each one of us has a responsibility. That responsibility refers to the individual cultivation of our relationship to earth and to spirit, to God. In this moment we may be able, if we wake up, to move beyond the endless waves of golden and dark ages on this planet. Due to the place of our consciousness as a species, and our relationship with the wider galaxy, we might awaken collectively to a more permanent remembrance. As part of this awakening, each one of us will be called to seek and find our spiritual root – to cultivate the spiritual identity which will carry us beyond time. In this body, we may learn, share, participate and embody multiple traditions. At the moment of our death, however, we will need a clear arrow to follow.

Because our opportunity to awaken is so great at this time I wish to reiterate the importance of several principles:

- Depth is a commitment to stand by the truths that we come to find are ours. To follow the path that we choose to its core. To utilise our power for creation of the good and the beautiful.

- Precision is a willingness to continually purify and clarify our total psycho-spiritual-body.
- Clear seeing, unencumbered by need, is to act from the heart as if we were walking on a tightrope where only truth will keep us standing.
- Imagination is our ability to create through first imagining that which we wish to live. We cultivate our imaginations through arts, music, dance, ritual and collective gathering.
- Beauty is a recognition that the beautiful is an integral part of the soul. It is both our duty and our responsibility to cultivate beauty, not just for ourselves, but for the next seven generations.

To me, these are key components to spiritual sovereignty.

I am aware that as I speak of these great ideals, and of our need to embody them, that stepping toward a sacred way of life may bring real issues and challenges to the forefront. For example, while religion has been necessary, to help some of us remember the sacred during our dark age, it has not been without fault. Religion, like all areas of life, has been corrupted. And so the time of religion will slowly fade. A universal esoteric platform will take its place. It will not look exactly like the shamanic, nomadic cultures of millennia past. And it will not look like the epochs of civilisations in relatively recent history. Our new life ways will be expressive of the truth of collective wakefulness and the vibration of universal love in its particular time.

Because this change is a moment of incredible opportunity and power, it is of vital importance that we do not bring polluted energies with us. As the power of this time begins to awaken us and move through us, it is natural that we will feel a rising of that power, known as kundalini, and with that an increase in our creative life force. Creation is a meeting of dark and light. And it is with care and precision that the meeting is managed toward beauty and health. There is so much more to be said about this topic than has already been mentioned but I will leave it simply: we know in our knowing when energies are not right. As part of our clearing, we are leaving behind energies of harm and abuse. At this time all of us have either experienced or know those who have experienced abuse. As kundalini rises there can sometimes be great confusion about what is pleasure and what is truth, but the truth is that we know in the depths of our knowing[1]. It is to the pure bright star of divine love in

---

1 Pleasure is not a source of shame, or something bad, in and of itself. It is a wonderful part of being human. However, spiritual traditions the world over teach that direct-

manifest union with our earthly forms that I appeal. As the future grandparents of the new way, we are the ones to guide the star of change. And change starts within. With our own creative life force.

We live in a culture of instant gratification. Because some of us have had access to food, shelter, clothing and entertainment without creating any of it ourselves, we seem to think that the fruits of our spiritual efforts will be known to us immediately. However, this goes against natural rhythms and cycles. It goes against the good of the whole to watch others suffer for our own indulgence. Golden Ages are not born of acquiescence. Golden Ages are born of purification, care and sustained effort. I remind us that we are moving within a vast experience of time. Time is speeding up, and changes are happening much faster than they have before. But this is in comparison to billions of years of geological change and more cultures than we can conceive of, all of which have come and gone. The movement out of our current dark age will likely take longer than our lifetimes. And so, we create beauty out of love for the coming generations.

As a collective, we may now be in the place where we can expand our notions of love into a spiritual outlook, one which is free from doctrine and judgement. A spiritual outlook which says, love is the basis of everything, a love more complete, more inclusive and more caring than we have dared to imagine so far. It's time we ask ourselves what is love, truly, when it is lived?

Spiritual Technologies

Our spiritual technologies are embodied and they are part of the foundation by which we come into unity. Technology can be seen from a number of perspectives both material and conceptual. At a material level, technology is a tool for the exchange of information, good and services. It is a tool for the creation of public and private space, for the care and transportation of bodies. Technology is a tool for almost any human endeavour. And while physical technologies of the contemporary period tend to depend on electricity, physical technologies of earlier periods tended to depend on craftsmanship and physical tools. Yet not all of our technologies are physical, and those that are most ancient are spiritual in their nature. Spiritual technologies are ontologies, and for this reason they are not often grouped with physical technologies. Spiritual technologies can use physical tools, such as the shoes made of nails worn by fakirs in India or beads used for mantra and prayer the world over, but more intrinsic

---

ing the sensual energies toward more elevated expression is vital to health, truth and spiritual evolution.

is their use of methods – methods of breathing, moving, thinking and being which facilitate or accelerate the development of the human.

Spiritual technologies were once, in previous golden ages, highly developed. They can and will be developed again. And as they are, they can be applied according to the truth, environment and heart of each community. For example, I see in the coming epoch networks of communities who pray around fires, communities who sing to the rising Sun, communities who nurture vast knowledges of permaculture, eco-design, sacred geometry, sacred sound. In each locale communities will discover and develop different sets of technologies for life which are reflective of their spiritual direction.

Technologies of the spirit can now emerge, because we are ready to apply them with care. The moment of trial and choice we are going through has the capacity to lead us to the centre of our hearts. And from our hearts, discovery happens. Remember, the outer is a reflection of the inner. So from this vantage point something like the internet is an outer reflection of the growing awareness of our interconnectedness. Our digital tools are but a reflection of the vast, light-speed capacities of our own imaginations. The virtual worlds are a reflection of the infinite subtle planes. Technologies stem from us at any moment in time in accordance with the capacities of our hearts. In this way, our 'need' for computers, phones and 'smart' technologies is already dissipating. As our ancestors before us, and as our children after us, we will navigate our walking and movement upon the Earth by feeling and knowing from our hearts. Telepathy is, for example, simply another way of receiving and processing information. Like all spiritual technologies, it is centred in the heart. As our hearts mature, our desire for the application of spiritual truths in our daily livedness can only lead to cleaner, more harmonious reflections from inner to outer world.

In a time when we are engaging online, separate but 'connected', we have an opportunity to reassess what connection is. And I would like us to consider that the body is an important part of connection. The electromagnetic frequencies of the body engage with one another on a cellular level through physical presence. This is why live interaction is so powerful. What is communicated is not of the mind alone, but on a cellular level we are exchanging information. The information that each of us carries within our cellular makeup, stemming from our path in this life and the stories we have encountered and the ways we have attended to those stories, is shared by being in presence with one another. In the spiritual dimensions, as well as online, we are indeed able to connect to the presences of others. However, it is only through the proximity of touch, taste and smell that certain qualities of information are shared.

And here we come again to the heart. The magnetic field of the heart has a physically measurable resonance of several meters. When we are in contact with each other, we naturally share our energies – hopefully for the positive. To go without such interaction is indeed unnatural for our psycho-spiritual-bodies. For it is in reflection through the other that we fully exist. How they see us, what they reflect back to us, is literally who we become.

To bridge our separation effectively, we are called to go deep within. This is the alchemical place where inner and outer search for harmony, for an equal and balanced mirror between the two. Spiritual technologies can help us to anchor the experience of our own heart. The more deeply we are anchored within, the more clear our outer reflections become. In this next epoch of humankind, where we move beyond separation and into unity, we will know with fullness and certainty how important we are to each other. To realise ourselves fully, as spiritual beings, spiritual community is important. A living tradition, with elders who are alive and part of a time-tested train of continuity, helps us greatly. Through such connections, we realise the pulsing reality of our one beating heart. Fluidly connected across our individual interweaving fields, we become anchored in physical presence by our gatherings.

Culture and Diversity

Unity through diversity means that diversity is an agent of change which catalyses unity. Unity is not homogeneous. Globalism, with its homogenising agents, leads not to unity, but to separation. Separation of the heart from the community, from its sense of connection to the qualities and beings which make it strong. Here I would like to speak from the Sufi path and the importance of culture that I have learned through it. For an Eastern mindset understands community in a way that is different from Europeans. Sufis understand the power of silent witness, of allowing, and of the way this moves deeper spiritual truths through individuals, impacting the whole of the community for the better. We hold each other in this way, lightly, and it is beautiful.

For example, the nefs, which are behaviours resulting from the immature ego, are something that need to be played out and seen, so that we can each make choices about them. The taming of the ego in this path does not have to be a hard endeavour, where we sit and look at ourselves with sternness or judgement. We simply live, and through the witness of those around us, we come to see ourselves and the impact of our behaviours on others. As we witness ourselves, we begin to feel. And from feeling, we are able, without judgement or criticism, just quietly, to make a change. As the change is perceived, we receive silent but encouraging reinforcement. Smiles. Occasionally a chat. And we see the flow of our communications and actions result in beauty rather than pain. This can be a slow process, so there is no rush. Each person is accepted exactly where they are, without shame, because it is better for them to be with the community rather than isolated. As we allow each other to be, to grow, in our own time and in our own way, we step outside of judgement, blame or the need to agree. Like flowers, we bloom, sometimes a small bloom, sometimes a bouquet. All is appreciated. And the witness of many, in ever so quiet a way, forms an interpersonal continuity.

Culture is necessary for cohesion. Without it, we may collide, each presenting or defending a certain viewpoint because it is what we have identified with or feel attached to. Culture, grown in harmony's expression, helps us to move beyond difference, while at the same time celebrating diversity. Cultures which are old, which come across time, and which have an imprint of harmony flowing through their activities have much to share with us. If we, as Europeans accustomed to individuality as a philosophical ideal, are able to relax the need for individual accolades, we may find that grounding ourselves within a culture allows a deeper individual expression to come through. An expression emplaced within others, within culture. For culture carries the dailiness of our interactions and gives them a set of structures by which the individual and community may enliven each other towards beauty.

Culture is necessarily local, because it grows through our daily interaction. As our lives become more localised, it is certain that new cultures will develop. This has always been the case, for culture is not static. The same old songs will have a feel, an expression to them, which is of the current moment. And we will mix. Peoples of the ancient world moved among each other. And because they were less interested in ownership and classification, they traded their wisdom and their practices freely. In this way, a breathing technique from India could be easily welcomed and utilised by an African seeker, and vice versa. As we move across the planet, encountering the cultures each one of us carries, we may share the imprints of beauty we carry between each other. A deep appreciation then ensues. An appreciation which does not need to own, commercialise or capitalise on that beauty. What occurs is a sharing of the moment of time, in which beauty is growing between us, in which we touch each other through our traditions. As people begin to settle in new communities, flavours and colours and textures will surely combine. And has this not always been the case? The deeper imprints move with us, finding expression in the now. And as we carry the deeper imprints with integrity and care, we ensure that they will flow again to the next generation and the next. We are not worried if our great, great grandchildren will have the notation exact. We are passing on a deeper set of truths. And because we care about those deeper truths, we will pass them on in the best detail we are able to, while allowing. This for me exemplifies reciprocity between past and future, and between peoples. Culture can then be seen as an agent of peace.

Trance and Transition

I awake this morning knowing that I am deeply afraid of transition. Despite all the work I do, in all the access to inner sight, I tend to power on like a warrior. Not to save anybody. Not to save myself. Just because it feels appropriate to do so. But in doing so I forget. I forget to feel. And feeling is feminine – for me. To make space for nothing. Nothing but being with what is. With no directionality. No high. No low. No thought. No emotion. Just the feeling of the energy as it is in its potent latency. Full in me. And that can be a scary place. Because the world of illusion, the world of maya, is full of flow. Maya is full of direction. Of thought. Of emotion. Manifestation. But potentiality is truth. And truth causes us to bow. So this is the real work. To bow. Each and every breath. To the totality of love. What is transition, but transition into greater and greater depths of truth. Further penetration and release into the heart of love. Birth. Death. Every breath. So in the bigger picture, this entire drama, this entire play, is just a way to learn to transition. Let us use it as a potent example then. An example for the soul. For the soul is here to learn. And to let go. (May 2021)

In the spiritual path, of all true traditions, death is an important foundation. In the Celtic shamanic paths, the initiate will be buried in the earth. They dig their own grave, enter it, are covered until only their face is open, and lie there overnight to die. In the Sufi tradition, the initiate will enter a dugout beneath the earth for 40 days. They remain in complete darkness, inside the belly of the Earth. Once a day they are delivered food and water. They die. And are reborn. There are further examples, but these are the traditions I know. In my own initiations, I go days with no food and no water. I sit up at night and sing, and pray. I lay down and enter the belly of the Earth through my imagination. And I die. And am reborn. I do this regularly. Because each moment is a living death, a living breath. And to remember love is to eventually be in a continual state of release and rebirth. Early on, I found death and birth practices through the dance form of Butoh. In Butoh we push the body beyond its extreme. We push it beyond exhaustion. We push it beyond habits. Beyond everything that it knows. And then, from the place of surrender, we move. In trance, through the thresholds of the subtle planes, Butoh dances us through birth, phases of childhood, mid-life, the autumn years, the winter years and death. Also in whirling, we move through trance into the subtle planes. Trance is an aspect of our capacity that predetermines our innate desire to die. The esoteric death – which is divine union. Death and spiritual union are one and the same. Complete spiritual union is the most ecstatic state a human can reach. But this has been misunderstood, in the age of doctrine and rule which got distorted with power mongering. Trance became vilified. Something to be afraid of. But actually, trance is our birthright. It is a powerful tool by which we move into our rebirth. A tool that needs to be treated with respect.

Trance is foundational of all true spiritual traditions. By true, I mean traditions that are tested by time – greater lengths of time than many would believe we have even existed for. Traditions founded on spiritual technologies that are not tied to belief[2]. Technologies which allow us to mature through phases of experience and knowing. Technologies practised by masters and handed down through direct contact. For millennia. We have an inborn desire for trance. And through trance, we experience ecstasy. Ecstasy is natural for the human being. A state of total connectedness. Not only did it help us to survive in nature, it amplified the power of our unique and beautiful human hearts. You see, when living in nature, we need to know when the trees will drop their leaves, when the animals will move inland, when the whales will grace us with their migrations. We need to know when the snow will fall, when the relatives from the village 10 hours' walking distance away will decide to visit. We need to know where fresh water emerges from the ground, and which herbs to take for healing wounds. And this knowledge, it comes through trance. Telepathy is not a mystery. It is simply a way of communicating across subtle realms. Realms that animals and plants are part of, for instance. Realms where frontal lobe cognition is not the primary space for knowing. Realms beyond words.

---

2 Here I speak to the yogic traditions of India and Tibet, founded on a science that works whatever the personal beliefs are. Some of the older shamanic traditions are similar in this way, in that their effects are measurable and real beyond the belief of the person. Belief is sometimes used in a way to speak of faith. However, there is a difference between blind belief and faith.

Where communication is very real, but more image-based, more feeling-based, and more direct. In older days, hunters were said to be in communication with the herds. The herds would offer up one of themselves to feed their human brothers and sisters. And the hunters would offer appropriate ceremony for the life of the animal. Deep reciprocity is part of telepathy. And deep reciprocity is part of trance. And this reciprocity is an aspect of trance that got buried and distorted in the age of power mongering. And the doctrinally based churches of recent history have been a part of this.

Oruç Güvenç (1948–2017) was a Sufi master in Turkey whose life focus was on music and trance. He understood, through the teachings of his own masters and life experience, that the traditions of Sufism came originally from Central Asia. They came from the base of the Himalayas so many generations ago. And they moved through space and time, through bodies, in a river of continuity that eventually ended up with the name of Sufism. Güvenç's life work was to trace this ancient music and to recreate the instruments. He produced a massive anthology of songs, ilahis and tunes that are precise and effective in their spiritual capacity. Re-cognising the psycho-spiritual-body in the same way as indigenous elders across the world, the science of music as a spiritual technology was refined and carried forward by Dr Güvenç. Other Sufi masters relate to music in a similar capacity. Hazrat Inayat Khan (1882–1927) spent a lifetime mastering the vina, an ancient lyre with the capacity to induce trance and healing through its simple melodies[3]. Khan wrote extensive treatises on the power of music, breath, sound and speech. According to Khan, the ancient sciences of sound and music are a part of any golden age. In the current epoch, music and sound are devolved so they are utilised simply for the purposes of moving a body, beating it like a machine. Breath and speech are understood and utilised for base communications. But as we cycle back into periods of golden ages, we naturally begin to remember and create more refined expressions (Khan, 2005).

The movement of the universe is ecstasy in motion. When we release ourselves into the movement of creation, we are in reciprocity, in harmony, with the natural and foundational matrices of life. For this reason, people may experience flow, or heightened states of awareness and focus, in any moment where

---

3 Hazrat Inayat Khan, quoted previously as well as here, was a Sufi master of the Chisti Order in India. Later in his life he developed a strong relationship with the West and the Inayati Order was formed.

their heart is in tune with their inner being and the world around them. As above, so below/as within, so without.

In our current moment in time, our forms of movement, thought and interaction are less refined. Our need for and our search for ecstasy are still alive within us however. And for this reason we see a number of different behaviours emerge culturally, some which cause harm and others which are simply misplaced or misunderstood. For example, a person, knowing they have a need for ecstatic experience, yet having no cultural grounding for it and no appropriate recourse to its healing and evolutionary manifestations, may seek out heightened states through the use of drugs. It is no coincidence that the collective global opening that occurred during the 1960s and 70s came on the back of the discovery of LSD. Lacking context and guidance however, that expansion soon deteriorated into the cultural use of cocaine, amphetamines, barbiturates, pills and a number of new synthetic methods for inducing peak experience. In a less harsh format, but equally unsatisfying, have been the seeking methods of 'New Age' spirituality, which has in many instances combined pills and synthetic drug use with basic spiritual technologies. These technologies include things like electronic sound scapes and sounding 'Aum' – the universal sound of creation, like dancing, or exhausting the body, or following sensation into the subtle dimensions[4]. What our globalised West has not culturally realised yet, however, is that such entry points can be like mirages, or distractions. For while they seem to abate our natural drive toward ecstasy, and lead to some expanded sense of connection with all that exists, such methods are not an end in themselves. If we, collectively, were to have access to true tradition and its powerful spiritual technologies, we would recognise the expanded states induced by chemicals, sex without love, and heightened experience without guidance as ultimately unrefined. We would naturally want to move beyond the world of senses into the subtle planes that are associated with death and rebirth.

We are collectively facing our fear of death in this moment. We are necessarily encountering a movement of transition. We are, in so many respects, undergoing a global, unified spiritual maturation process. And as part of this our intuitive, telepathic and ecstatic capacities will begin to open. For some, this will begin as a subtle strengthening of intuition. For others, states previously attained only by sages will become more readily available. For example,

---

4 Sound scapes and dancing are themselves very good tools. My point is to not get lost at the gate – and to not pollute it. I was once reminded, however, by an eminent festival director, that even the kid in the ball cap chewing gum all night is somewhere on his journey. We all begin wherever we can.

in yogic traditions, those who enter the deepest trance states arrive into ecstatic postures as part of the journey into the subtle planes. In meditative traditions one enters trance while seated and still, where an astral body becomes alive and materially manifest in the subtle dimensions. In the Sufi tradition, trance can be visually seen when the dervishes whirl, expressing the inner union they experience through the geometric principle of a whirling form. Through *dhikr*, also known as *mantra*, *wazifa* or chanting, we enter trance. We may also enter these gates through simple prayer. Sacred music is one of the best catalysts, however, because it brings with it joy, sadness and all the qualities of humanity which rise and fade away in our alchemical journeys. In the most subtle of experience, the breath and intention alone can carry the soul through all manner of worlds. How we engage our newfound openings into the ecstatic dimensions is of ultimate importance in this moment.

What Is it Like

Windmills dot the hills. A clear blue sky expands in all directions. Birds sing. The ocean gently laps the shores. A palpable peace hangs in the air, touches the skin, breathes through the people. And we are gathered in groups. We share culture – music, song, technologies. There is food growing, and medicine. Incredible healing takes place every day. An incredible love moves between us. And this does not mean that there is no conflict or that there are no stages to maturity. It does not mean we are all perfect. The peace and love we share simply indicate that we have let go of our previous age and have fulfilled our role in creating an age of togetherness. Our communities are small enough to be places where we know each other. And large enough that we are free to grow, explore, to leave and to return. We are connected, community to community. We celebrate our differences. We are not afraid of the community across the land or water. We are anchors of love, shepherding each other into wholeness, midwifing each other through death and birth. (August 2014)

These are my visions. Over the years I have looked consistently into the future. I have asked, what must we do now, and what is our inevitable end as human beings? And each time, despite all the chaos I have seen around me, I see that the future is bright. Bright and full of light, in the eyes and the hearts of the Earth's beings. They have shiny skin and shiny hair. The air is clean and good. The sky is bluer than blue. And the water is flowing freely, with a mighty song and voice that echoes through the cosmos.

To move from A to B an inner imagination is crucial. As humans created in the image of God, we are creators and creatrix. As women give birth to physical life, all humans give birth to themselves and to the world they inhabit. We are stewards of this planet as dreamers and lovers. When the human loves the Earth and cares for her as a true maternal archetype, she blossoms. When the creation blossoms her people live in abundance and harmony. Beauty, once again, emerges as central to the existence of life on Earth. And for beauty to come into fruition, we must dream. And so, dear reader, I implore you now to imagine with all of your heart. What we bring through the imaginal realms, invigorated in the heart, flows through us into existence.

What do the new life ways look like for you? What do they feel like? What is the medicine of your heart, anchored through your body? Who are you living with? Which community sings just for you? What are your practices? Where is your garden? Where do you plant your feet? Does your heart say be still? Does it ask you to learn an instrument, plant a seed, steward the growth of something shared? The time is now to listen to that voice. Now is the time to let go and to act on your inner knowing.

In the moment of now we are creating the mythologies that will sustain the next seven generations. It is important to carry the river of our traditions across time, and it is important to find and create fresh expressions of the current moment. These fresh expressions become the stories, the legend, the myth of our great, great, great, great, great, great, grandchildren. These expressions become a road from the future back to the prayers of this moment. A road by which our spirits and our love may pass from now into the seeds of our descendants' dreams. We do not need to create monuments to glorify ourselves in stone or towers. We can create instead dances, songs, stories and prayers that are alive with the sacred breath of our souls. Just as our ancestors have before us. For it is through their insight and expression that our sacred technologies are with us, to carry us back to remembering. Because our ancestors took the love and care in their beings, and extended themselves through the writing of the vedas, the creation of our mantras, the careful crafting of sacred music and movements, we now have foundations we can stand on, if we choose to do so. And should we not do the same? Shall we not carry forward the spiritual technologies of millennia past, adding to them the vibrancy and lessons of our time? Shall our children not bear witness to our learnings, that they may be secure in their own development and maturation processes?

In Search of a Vision

The most profound ideas in a culture and society necessarily engage the moment, the ones that have lasting power have a forward momentum. It is my desire, after bringing various perspectives together, to look at ways of moving forward. We have looked at food sovereignty as a critical issue for survival and the continuation of life. We have looked at nuclear disarmament in the same vein. And we have looked at resilience through our faith, hope, and our willingness to take full responsibility for the way we live. In terms of wisdom from deep traditions, carried across time and through different places, what is shared here is but a small part. What is handed down beyond the written word, the oral tradition, is that which comes through rites and rituals, through blood and bone memory. I hope what I have shared is just enough to open a conversation between your heart and mind, dear reader, and to touch your life. The transition we are looking at is perhaps bigger than we can actually comprehend. So it is my hope that you will find within these pages what you need to continue this important conversation – form communities of resilience and joy for yourself and those around you. For the continuation of life is the bigger picture we are looking at, from so many vantage points.

Moving forward, we can take steps to connect to Earth, find our vision and embody joy. Floyd Red Crow Westerman (1936–2007), a beloved Dakota singer, actor and activist, has spoken:

I try to bring something to everybody's thinking. I always think we should be on the same page but we're not…The Europeans came with the Bible. And in the Bible it says very little about the Mother Earth as sacred. There's a very crucial absence of thinking that they didn't think Mother Earth was sacred enough to mention. And the absence of that has got us into this polluted world. And our children have no future because of this. For Indian people, to all of us, the Earth is our Bible. (2008)

Westerman was a joyful human being: he created beautiful music and he also spoke his truth with clarity. He encouraged Americans and the rest of the world to look into Indian spirituality for the purposes of opening our minds so that we might understand what the Earth is saying.

In a slightly different but similar vein, Karen Schafer, who channels a being she knows as White Eagle[5], writes:

---

5 I include this message from Schafer because it speaks to a universal truth which is

My heart weeps with yours. But Joy comes in the morning.

Deep joy underlies all the sorrow, carries anew all the tears, sweeps them into a river of life so beautiful – more beautiful than you could ever know. You speak of rapture but there is no rapture as beautiful as this – that one's love is transformed into myriad pieces of Pure Joy, into myriad lines of Love that spread well beyond the universe you know.

Follow the thread! See what happens! See how beautifully Love commands the Field!

Your tears of love swell into a river of joy, rejoicing in the life that is now and is forever. Think not that they are dead whom you have loved. All their love for you has been transmuted into a far finer vibration of love that surrounds you always, that lifts you up, that brings you inner joy, that reminds you of life everlasting.

Yes, the flow of tears is continual, but it swells the vibration of the planet, bringing it ever higher into vibrations of Love – Swells of Well-Being, Waves of Delight! Do you not see? How beautiful is the World of Light in which you can dance to your heart's content – for all join you in the Light – the Light Everlasting, dancing joyously, celebrating the beauty of Life beyond knowing.

Ancient footsteps precede you, showing you the way into the Light, for there is no shadow that can withstand the glory of the Light, the beauty of who you are, the cleansing of your tears, the removal of any shadow of doubt. Our hearts weep with yours but in a manner so profound, well beyond your understanding. Listen to your heart and let it speak of joy amid the tears. Let it remind you of Life, that lives forever.

Weep not! For our hearts are swelled with Love and your Joy is imminent. It is here – within you. Gently, gently see beneath the tears, for your tears have created a Well of Understanding – and deep within that Well, you will find Wisdom – the Wisdom of Love, the Wisdom of Joy, the Wisdom of Peace.

---

the mystical relationship of joy and sorrow. When reading channelled messages it is important to have discretion. Truth can be found everywhere, and finding a living elder to help make sense keeps us grounded. The teachings I have received on joy and sorrow, through my own Sufi journey, are inwardly quite profound.

And knowing that, you are All Well, you are All at Peace, you are All One in wholeness, in loving care, in serene beauty. Nothing, nothing can obscure that Understanding, that Wisdom, that Joy, that Love, that Peace. (2021)

A vision is a gift from the divine, a guiding light for ourselves and our community. Where can you find the one that you will carry? How do you know who to trust in this climate? In brief, the person you must trust most is yourself. Your feeling is the feeling to follow. What it truthfully says, when you are able to access it. And if you cannot access it, that is your first quest. To become still, in your heart, and ask to hear. There are many resources. These days you can learn to meditate through an app or many free videos and resources. You can teach yourself to breathe by simply observing your breath for 5–15 minutes each day. You can start to walk to experience nature. You can attend yoga classes online or in person. There are many ways to begin. And once you are ready, you can find an elder or a teacher whom you feel inside that you can trust. Remember to trust yourself, and your ability to make your own choices. Make the commitment to look after yourself, to centre yourself, to do the best you can. And the doors will open.

A teacher is helpful, to bring you through the difficult parts of the process of transformation. A guide who has walked their path themselves can encourage you and look out for you when you need it. It is said, 'when the student is ready the teacher appears'. So again, trust.

As your vision develops, begin to live it. In the indigenous perspective, it is not necessary that we share the details of our visionary experience with other people. Sharing the details of our visions can actually dilute them. The most potent and effective course of action to manifest our visions is to fully live them. Put the energy into living them. And watch how your life changes. Each one of us is vibrantly vital to the solutions for our local space and place. What works for our community, our neighbourhood, our environment, may not work anywhere else on the planet. If it works, if the people are healthy, if they are comfortable, harmonious, abundant, then it is a good set of solutions.

It is OK, amidst the great suffering across the planet, to thrive and to experience joy. There is joy in learning to grow food. There is joy in emptying our hearts to loves surrender. Joy is OK because it is necessary. We do not have to resign ourselves to anything less than joy. Because when we take responsibility to create it, then joy is the fruit of the efforts of our hearts. To see each other joyful is a wonderful thing indeed! And it is a powerful ingredient in dissolving poison.

Seeds Take Time

Sufism, like Vedanta, has a long tradition of scholarship and debate. There are numerous complete and distinct systems of thought within each tradition. And each system leads to a well of beauty and truth. The purpose of the systems has been to provide pathways by which the soul of a student may mature. Spiritual maturity, like physical maturity, takes time. We apply ourselves, and are tested by life. And when we have a system, tradition or structure to help guide us, our trials may be easier to pass. We may come to peace more assuredly.

Such traditions are called perennial, because they speak to the perennial questions of existence. They are philosophies in that they comprise living and breathing ontologies. The vedas, long before they were written down, were lived, refined and passed down orally for unknown ages of mankind. Scholars of Vedanta themselves believe that the tradition could be as old as millions of years. For the Vedic cosmologies do not place the origin of human life within the current period alone, but across the vast expanse of geological existence on the planet. We, according to the Vedic elders, have been here with the Earth, a part of her, for more ages than we can even recall. We have become nearly extinct so many times, and each time a new world began out of that process.

From a perennialist view, the changes we are undergoing now may not be reversible. This is not because we as a collective body of humans are not picking up our mess fast enough – but rather because the trajectory of growth that we are on must now complete its cycle of birth, life, death and rebirth. According to perennial scholars, the period we are living in now is simply the result of seeds that were sown thousands upon thousands of years ago. Through these seeds, whole forests were formed. And each seed that grew released more seeds. Until the whole of the world was covered. Not in peace, or abundance, or truth. But rather in fear, division and war. To resolve the present circumstance, we must plant different seeds. And nourish them, protect them, teach our children to help them grow. Just as the issues we are facing took thousands of years to fully reveal themselves, the solutions which neutralise may take an equally long time to grow. To learn to love again, to respect, to live in reciprocity with each other, as families and communities – these are all seeds that we are really just now imagining. Through the spread of yoga and meditation across the world, we are collectively joining our hearts and minds toward the possibilities of new seeds. Through the rise of a global shamanic culture, we are tilling our ground for planting. Yet only a few seeds are formed enough to be planted just yet. Many of us are still wrapped in war, division and fear. Either through our thinking or life circumstance, or both. And for this we cannot judge each other or ourselves. This is a dense forest we have been born into, and our thinking has been conditioned from a very early age. If we re-cognise however, that the qualities in our hearts wanting to burst through are the actual and real antidote and solution, that is a big, big step in a better direction. We can nourish qualities that form themselves into seeds of love. This is something each of us can do. For those who have been able and willing have carefully been keeping the seed beds ready. To re-dream the land and our relationship to it would be a perennial solution. Gardens take care and grace and time to grow. But with these things they do. A beautiful future is possible.

A Golden Transformation

While we are part of a larger mathematical unfolding, it is my personal view that golden ages occur when the humans on Earth collectively enter more refined golden states of being. Outer reflects inner. Below reflects above.

We are all undergoing change and transformation. The personal and the collective are intertwined. The flow of our consciousness and being flows and migrates according to its natural rhythms and cycles. Within this larger flow, our personal lives are created, our stories spun. The power of the human heart cannot be underestimated. All creatures are sentient, and wise. The human heart, however, has the power to create, through its frequency and emotion. Through the focus of the heart, the dream of life unfolds. This has been said in so many different ways across the text. Here, I draw our attention to the power of the heart in transformation, as an engine of our transition.

To transform the leaden into copper, the copper into gold, is a process of continual refinement. There is a core of knowledge held within spiritual traditions that is true, tested by time, passed down from before the ages of writing and civilisation. This core of knowledge is safeguarded by an inherent property of protection. And that property is love. Divine love is the only agent which will activate the inner and spiritual knowledges fully. And so we are drawn to it.

The masters and teachers of our great traditions are masters because they guide us to the love which ignites the truth of the heart. Here I am talking about the great love and the great truth and the great work. Our reason for being born. There are many kinds of love, and as an ideal, all forms of love can and do lead us to the great love. This process is also known as the science of alchemy. The science of creating the philosopher's stone, or turning base matter into gold.

In Sufism, there are four main stages to the soul's alchemical process. These include first finding the path, the outer way, the major signposts which come to you in your life and direct you toward the inner journey. The second stage is then discovering the specific family group, spiritual system and set of practices and people with whom you will know community and journey. The third stage is the opening of mystical and inner truth within. This is where the heart begins to come alive. It is the stage of ecstatic experience and inner knowledge igniting. The fourth stage is then union with love. Lover, or human, and beloved, become inseparable. The names of these stages in Turkish are: *shariat*, *tariqat*, *marifat* and *haqiqat*. Within the stages are also many stations, which could be seen as resting points or mile markers. Our journey never truly ends until the last breath, but along the way there are many milestones of spiritual maturity.

I appreciate the stages of change as they are understood and moved through in Sufism. Each one is rich in layers, with many textures and tides. It is universal within the stages to encounter an opening to grief – a deep, universal grief. At some point we find a powerful sense of bliss and of belonging – and yet at the same time we will learn to let go of attachment and desire. We learn to face our fears, and through doing so experience true surrender. In the process of change, many parts of ourselves will die. And we may even have the experience that we are dying – without actually physically dying – at various points in our journey. Like grapes being pressed through a sieve, the waves of our transformation slowly separate the coarse outer skin of our being from the fine, inner fruit. As we marinate in the juices of our practices and life, we slowly ferment and ripen. Eventually, we become as fine wine.

Equally effective are the Yogic, Buddhist and Shamanic paths, in which I have some interest. Each of these includes – with different emphasis – the return of the soul, the taming of the ego, the awakening of the heart, living in truth, standing up in community, and rites of death and spiritual passage. Each will lead through its vast root system to the source of divine love and union. Each will stand its place in the universal esoteric platform through you, the people who by their devotions and transformations, embody them fully.

Neurological Change
The body is an incredible agent for our developmental change.

Irina Tweedie, a student of the Sufi path who wrote extensively about her initiatory experience, describes the process of change as swimming, 'always throwing water behind you' (2014). By this she meant that we are never the same one moment to the next. We are always changing, always evolving. Maturation does not always stop to consider itself. It lives, it breathes. We are constantly reborn.

We are psycho-spiritual-bodies in a process of continual change. Therefore, the systems of our body are holographic. The breath exchanges toxins and water vapours for oxygen. The blood, as it moves through cell walls and nerve endings, releases minerals for absorption while at the same time mopping up acids and other wastes. The kidneys and liver absorb wastes and compost them into urine and bile, which are then recycled for the breakdown of fats. In a similar way, the grooves of our cortical matter can be continuously wiped down and made elastic. And the way we think, move and behave affects the shape our brains and bodies take. For example, breathing happens naturally, but there are many techniques which direct the breath in certain cleansing, relaxing or restorative functions. We may consciously shape the breath toward more refined processes. In advanced meditation, we learn to slow the heart, thus allowing for fuller volumes of exchange within the tissues. And in the cortical brain, we may, through the use of spiritual technologies, direct and refine the way we receive and process information. This latter process is known in scientific terms as neurological tuning.

Neurological tuning is the process by which the grooves, or information highways, of our brain are created. As infants and children, our initial responses to stimuli form the basis of our neurology. At about the age of two we begin to differentiate and again around the age of 12. At each of these junctures, as well as at moments of heightened emotional experience, the brain reconfigures itself. As we respond to both external stimulus, and internal, or memory-based stimulus, we deepen grooves of neocortical matter. When we have regular, protected opportunities to encounter ecstatic states, our brain matter functionally changes shape. Our response patterns thus shift, allowing us to act more directly from the heart.

Neurological tuning is fascinating to consider because it provides a key to awakening our sovereignty. As we enter the subtle realms, the grooves of our cognitive tissues are entrained toward this direction. In this way, we become aligned with our spirit and soul. Nothing stands between the individual and their experience of the divine. They are free to move within the subtle realms

– closer and closer to love. The practices which move us to these thresholds are practices of trance.

Trance is our birthright. It has been muddied, shamed and imprisoned by both religious and government powers, and increasingly by corporate powers and a medical industrial complex. Trance is a power so true that the individuals who move into its realms must be looked after. And for this we have time-tested spiritual technologies and teachers. To spiritually evolve, the human must learn to find their own inner source of knowing, and their own powerful connection to the deepest source of love. Through protected, well travelled paths of initiation, we become spiritually sovereign. An individual is then able to stand in their own truth and bring the essence of their individual medicine to culture and society.

As part of the natural, bigger changes happening in the Earth's cycles, we are physically changing. We are embodied beings. And there are exchanges taking place from person to person whenever we are together. The embodied knowledge of our movements into the subtle planes is carried with us as we walk, talk, and engage. These knowledges are communicated person to person through our proximity and sharing. It is therefore important that we gather with others who are also on a path of alchemy. And it is important that we sit together to exchange conversation, practices, mantra and meditation. In a moment of geological, cosmological and embodied transition such as this one, it is simply vital that we reflect back to each other the fullness of our expansion. Consciousness evolves through interaction. And we can choose how that process unfolds. We have the capacity to tune and entrain our full, psycho-spiritual-physical selves to divine love.

Summation

In this writing we have looked at prophecy, philosophy, indigenous and contemporary thought. We have drawn a little from spiritual masters and teachings. And I have asked you reader, to step into a world of possibility, which is also a world of individual sovereignty. I have asked you to take responsibility for your own process of spiritual maturation, to move confidently toward your own next step, with eyes wide open. And that is a huge ask. It is huge because it is not what the dominant culture is asking of you. And that is because the culture that is dominant right now is the result of seeds that are nearing the end of their lifetime. The process of change is at first an individual process. As more and more people open their eyes to the deeper currents flowing in this moment, our attention will shift from the old to the new. And as this happens, collective creation will begin to take place. This is known as a mass shift in consciousness. It has happened before, and it is certainly possible now, because the river of transformation and change we are in is bigger than us. When we, as a collective body, are as refined as pure gold within our souls, the golden ages will then arrive. For they are a reflection of our collective heart.

In the next chapter we look at ways you can support your own transformative journey. Wherever you are in your stages, you can be supported by daily practice. The psycho-spiritual-body is not separate. So whatever you do on a physical level has an implication for your spirit. And whatever refinements you make on a spiritual level, they will in time become manifest on the physical plane.

Part 3

Chapter Six

Self Care

We Are Creators

Our covenant
Our breath is our covenant with Creator.
Changing Woman, who created us out of her skin
Became the womb of the Earth,
The earth receiving the Sun.
They are the mother and the father
Of all beings on Earth.

The great spiritual father – the central spiritual Sun – the word
The word is the father, the word became movement, breath and light.
The great spiritual mother – the queen of heaven – the creatrix
She who is nothing, from her impulse the word was spoken.

We love the great mother and we love the great father.
We love the Earth mother and are seeds of the Sun
We thank them for our earthly life.
Then we connect to the queen of heaven, the great impulse
And we enact the role of the central spiritual Sun – the great father
This is what it means to be created in the image of God.

Our breath is our covenant with Creator
Our breath speaks life into being.
Hannah Jewel

Indigenous cultures remember that we are created in the image of God, by the fact that we are creators. In the oldest of days, before written and even oral traditions, we did not speak so much. We observed, we felt, and we acted. Speaking was not a mode of communication, but a mode of creation. Right now, as our life force, our breath, comes to the height of our focus – we by necessity anchor into deeper, older knowledges. Our knowledges are born afresh from the expanse within. The fathomless remembering has waited to return until our hearts became purified enough to hold it. The seed of our essence is now exposed. And our reactions to this exposure are diverse.

For you, what does it feel like to crack open? Do you have physical sensations, visions – are you having dreams? As your heart starts to be seen, what does it say? What long pent-up stories and feelings need to be attended to? What new directions and ideas spring from the essence of your heart's truth? Where are your tears and where does your joy shine forth? How does your body communicate to you? What happens when you listen?

Breathing and Counting Exercises

The following two exercises are to help slow down and clear the mind. Before we do anything else, it's important to pause and feel centred. Simple but powerfully important.

You may read through each exercise and then do the exercise from memory. Or you might record yourself reading the instructions on a voice memo to play back. It's good to hear yourself speak.

When you are ready to begin, make a safe space, where you will not receive notifications or interruptions. A clean space is good. If you feel, you can light a candle or burn an incense. Just to be in a safe, clean space is enough.

1. **Lengthening the Breath.** 10 minutes.
   In this exercise you will feel your brain waves slow until the point that you are in a deep but waking rest. As you remain in the resting state your body will restore itself.

   - Get comfortable, seated on a chair, cushion or on the floor.
     Feel your sitting bones rooted into the ground.
     Allow your shoulders to drop, your hands to become heavy.

   - Breathe in deeply through the full torso.
     Allow your head to float toward the sky.
     Breathe out fully, lengthening the spine.

   - Breathe in for a count of *six* seconds.
     Pause briefly at the top.

And breathe out for a count of *six* seconds.
Pause briefly at the bottom.

- Continue the *six* seconds per inhale and *six* seconds per exhale for at least five minutes.

- When you have reached a state of total stillness, allow your breathing to return to normal.
Stay in the deep state until you naturally come out of it.

2. **Breath for Mental Clarity.** To calm anxiety. 10 minutes.
In this exercise you will feel your body grounding, it will become easier to let go. You will feel more solid on the Earth but full of life.

- Get comfortable, seated on a chair, cushion or on the floor.
Feel your sitting bones rooted into the ground.
Allow your shoulders to drop, your hands to become heavy.

- Breathe in deeply through the full torso.
Allow your head to float toward the sky.
Breathe out fully, lengthening the spine.

- Breathe in for a count of *seven* seconds.
Pause briefly at the top.
And breathe out for a count of *eleven* seconds.
Pause briefly at the bottom.

- Continue the *seven* seconds per inhale and *eleven* seconds per exhale for at least five minutes.

- When you have reached a state of calm, allow your breathing to return to normal.
As you slowly come out of the quiet state, perceive the room or environment around you – be aware of your inner sense of clarity.

Respiration

Primary respiration is the metaphysical mechanism by which we maintain a spirit within a body. Secondary respiration is the physical mechanism through which our breath creates existence. Together they form a covenant of life between our earthly mother and father, and our greater mother and father.

Respiration is fundamental to existence. Humans can, with great inner fortitude, live up to 40 days without food[1]. We can live three days without water, provided we know how to recycle our own fluids. Without breath, however, we can only survive two minutes. And while deep sea divers may be able to hold their breath for 20 minutes, they are still engaging all the elemental expressions of respiration. Two–three minutes without respiration is fatal.

In the exchange of gases, respiration functions under the air element. Air is a mixture of moisture, movement and molecular combinations. Breath, air, and breathing in this way have similar counterparts in all of the elements – water, earth and fire. In the exchange of nutrients and waste through the blood systems, respiration functions under the water element. In the management/recycling/composting systems of the digestive system, respiration functions under the earth element. And in the exchange of light and electromagnetic impulses, the visionary and sensory/motor systems rule the fire expressions of respiration. In this way conventional, or Western ideas about respiration meet the more ancient knowledges of Eastern systems, which still retain a holistic root.

Primary respiration is the spiritual breath of life – that which animates the soul and which breathes a being alive. In my own experience, I feel primary respiration as a pulsating movement in the crown chakra of the head. In Ayurvedic terms it is known as prana, in Chinese medicine – chi and in Reiki – ki. It is the spiritual breath of life, the ensoulment of the being. Primary respiration is in continuous flow even without our awareness. The more aware we become of it, the more freely it will flow. This is the respiration that moves through us with subtle yet powerful life force. When secondary respiration is in danger, primary respiration can be focused on as an anchor for life.

The following exercises work through secondary respiration to activate the primary. They may be done individually or in the order presented. As a group they move you through a gentle standing breath, a vigorous breath, and a seated integrated breathing pattern.

Standing Ha Breath: Stand with the feet directly underneath the pelvis. Raise the arms to shoulder height and turn the palms upward. Cross the arms in

---

1 It is known that mystics the world over fast for up to 40 days as part of their initiations. In more drastic accounts, there are saints and sages who give up food for decades, or even a lifetime (Yogananda, pp. 505–517).

front of the chest in a rhythmic movement, opening them out to the side again. Repeat, adding the breath. Breath out through the nose as the arms cross one over the other and switch. Then in through the nose as the arms raise to the side. Repeat at least 10 times but up to 20 or 30 as desired. End with a gentle shake of the body to release. (Chitty and Muller, 1990)

Breath of Fire: Kneeling on the knees or standing, reach the hands to the sky. Fold the four main fingers on each hand and keep the thumb pointing up. Breathe in through the nose while pulling the belly button in toward the spine. Release the belly and allow the inhale to happen, also through the nose. Repeat the breathing pattern, going as slow or as fast as you like, for at least two minutes. At the end take a large cleansing breath, shake out the body and smile.

Sufi Elemental Breath: Come to a comfortable seated posture. Spend two to ten minutes with each of the four breaths below. As you complete the breaths you will be in a deep state. Stay there until you naturally emerge.

1. In through the nose out through the mouth (air)
2. In through the mouth out through the mouth (earth)
3. In through the mouth out through the nose (water)
4. In through the nose out through the nose (fire)

The Chakra System

One of the largest, most simple maps of the human energy field is the chakra system. The seven major chakras rest along the spine. Each centre spins anticlockwise from the front of the spine and clockwise from the back of the spine. As they spin out they form our arms and legs, fingers and toes. As the chakra centres spin they exchange subtle information with the environment on all levels. This is physical, emotional, mental and spiritual. Our bodies talk to each other through these centres. For example, it is a colloquial expression to say 'Our hearts are talking to each other'. They are. The electromagnetic field of the heart can be physically measured several metres in either direction of a person and can be felt by another being even halfway across the globe.

The chakras are often depicted as geometries or flowers. Each centre is said to have a certain number of petals, with the crown, or soul chakra having a thousand petals to its lotus blossom. The study of the chakras is extensive, for it is an ancient metaphysical knowledge passed down long before the written word. There are many descriptions and depictions. As with all things, feel into your own experience of your chakras to allow your own remembering to emerge. For example, I experience the crown chakra as having millions of petals and the heart as an ever-unfolding lotus system.

In addition to the major chakras there are many minor chakras. The maps of these systems are extensive and there are whole healing systems associated with each. Additionally, there are cross-over and equivalent maps in other systems, such as Chinese medicine and Tibetan healing. Indeed, most indigenous healing systems will have developed a complete understanding of the human energy system.

Cleansing the chakra system is a good way to clean the associated energies of each centre. When we cleanse the chakras we cleanse our physical, emotional, mental and spiritual bodies. Many places where we feel stuck, or where stagnation has taken root in the body, can be alleviated through a regular, daily cleanse of the chakra system.

Water Cleansing for Chakras

Stand in the shower or under a waterfall. Breathe deeply in and out 10 full times. When you are ready, turn the water to cold.

- Stand with the front of your pelvis in the main stream of the water. Focus on a good cleanse of the sacral and pelvic centres. Breathe deeply. Then step away from the water.
- Re-enter the stream of water and stand with the belly under the main stream of water. Focus on a good cleanse of the solar plexus centre. Breathe deeply. Then step away from the water.
- Re-enter the stream of water and stand with your heart in the main stream of the water. Focus on a good cleanse of the heart centre. Breathe deeply. Then step away from the water.
- Re-enter the stream of water and stand with your face in the water. Focus on a good cleanse of the throat and third eye centres. Breathe deeply. Then step away from the water.
- Re-enter the stream of the water and stand with the top of your head in the stream of the water. Focus on a good cleanse of the soul centre. Breathe deeply. Then step away from the water.

Allow the body to rest a minute, and then repeat, placing the back of the spine in the stream of running water.

- Stand with the sacrum under the water, focusing on the sacral centre. Breathe deeply. Then step away from the water.
- Stand with the lumbar spine, focusing on the pelvic centre. Breathe deeply. Then step away from the water.
- Stand with the mid back, focusing on the solar plexus centre. Breathe deeply. Then step away from the water.
- Stand with the tops of the shoulders under the water, focusing on the heart and throat centres. Breathe deeply. Then step away from the water.
- Stand with the top of the head under the water, focusing on the third eye and soul centres. Breathe deeply. Then step away from the water.

Allow the body to rest a minute, and repeat as many times as feels productive. I find that, after using the sauna or swimming, I like to do three rounds of this cleansing. Make sure you warm the body afterwards by wrapping in a towel or bathrobe. You may also wish to cover the head with a comfortable woolly hat. While we have focused the energies with the cold water to cleanse them, we now want to bring the energy out to the whole of the body through warmth.

Smudging

Smudging is an ancient practice which utilises a play between positive and negative ions in smoke to cleanse the magnetic field of your energy body. As I understand it, negative ions in the electromagnetic field will naturally attract the positive ions of the smoke. As the smoke lifts away, so do the negative ions. This leaves you physically cleansed, and the sweet smell of the incense acts as a blessing, providing grounding and a sense of goodness to your sensory system.

You will need a candle and an aromatic, cleansing smudge. You will want a clean, tidy space. As you smudge yourself, do not touch the body directly with the burning or smoking smudge. Simply allow the smoke itself to caress the auric field and skin.

Take your bundle of sagebrush, stick of Palo Santo, or a regular incense stick. Light it with your candle or from the ember of a fire. Stand with your feet firmly upon the earth.

- Spread your toes, centre and ground your body. Take the smudge bundle, stick or incense and begin to cleanse from the top of the head along the top of the arms.

- Continue in a motion from the midline, or centre of the body, to the periphery. Move from each chakra centre, along the feathers of your 'wings' and to their edge.
- Do this for each side of the body. Then move down the legs front and back.
- Pick up each foot and smudge underneath it.
- Place the smudge between your legs and allow the smoke to rise to the sacral centre.
- Then move the smudge in a circular motion at each chakra centre up the front of the spine.
- Repeat to the back.
- As you circle the final soul chakra at the top of the head, focus on gratitude for all that you have carried. Thank it and wish it well as it departs.

Smudging, like water cleansing, can be done every day for good effect.

Allowing the Current to Pass Through

The other night I went for a walk in the moonlight. With most of the people in their houses, I was alone with nature. Sparking memories from my childhood, when I would often sit up at night, communing with trees and talking with the moon, I felt again an innocence which is central to the Earth. She is mother, she is in tune with the energies of infancy and childhood, as well as those of adolescence and maturity. She can be playful as she can be fierce. Her resting point is in the long tidal rhythms of early childhood. These rhythms have a neutrality to them that is refreshing to the soul.

I stood by the river. I stood there and looked up at the Moon. The branches of a birch were silhouetted, new leaves just ready to spread out. I asked mother, how do you carry this, all of our chaos, all of our noise? She spoke gently and said. 'Observe, it passes through me. I am never dormant. I am resting, yet I never sleep. In constant transmutation. This is what my children require of me, and so I do it.' (April 2020)

Our bodies are made of earth. And we too are in a state of constant transmutation. We can purify in many ways – sweating, fasting, elimination of wastes via the bowels and urine. We can get a fever. We can vomit. We release through sound, trembling – through tingling, heat and cold. These all support the body in its natural cleansing process. In the passage above I was feeling strongly the electrical current as it passed through.

Remember Arthur Firstenburg and the symptoms and causes of electricity poisoning (Chapter 1). While most of us will not experience extreme effects, it is good nonetheless to recall their known progression:

- Headaches
- Muscle cramps – begins first in small muscles and later in large muscle groups
- Shortness of breath – appears randomly and not necessarily with exercise
- Rising temperature – feels as if the blood is boiling
- Neurological meltdown – feels like the brain is melting, can come and go in waves
- Paralysis – this can look like seizures
- Rapid cell die-off – As cells die they excrete waste and this waste can materialise in any of the possible vectors out of the body, including lungs, intestines and facial orifices. Appears as mucus.

Unless there is a storm of unprecedented power, the electrical grid is likely to continue to increase. The use of satellites to create a global grid may lead to overexposure in some people.

Lay on the Ground

One of my favourite practices, taught to me by a Cherokee elder, is to lay upon the Earth. We lay down on our side, and we release ourselves into her body. Sinking below the earth, we allow our bodies to dissolve, for all to pass through us and into the body of our mother, into soil. When we are well below the surface of the Earth, in our energetic and spiritual bodies, we will finally come to a place of emptiness. Then, like the tender shoots of early spring, we begin to respirate upwards toward the surface. Arriving back fully into our bones we feel their weight upon the ground. We give thanks. We give great and deep thanks to our mother, who has taken and cleansed the flesh.

Earth Yourself

You can literally earth yourself as you go about your daily life. You may wear magnetic, copper and silver jewellery to physically ground the system.

You may get or create earthing sheets, which are lined with silver. The cyclists of the Tour de France use earthing sleeping bags for support and to cleanse the current generated by cycling on a road all day for weeks and months at a time.

Stay outside and walk barefoot as much as possible. Twenty minutes a day is recommended as a minimum.

Nutritional Support

Purify the blood. The less waste there is in the blood to begin with the easier your body will be able to cope. Excellent blood purifiers include dandelion root, red clover blossoms (my favourite), and the needles of blue spruce, Scots pine, Douglas fir, coastal redwood and Ponderosa pine. All can be made as tea or infusions.

To strengthen the heart make a tea or tincture out of hawthorn berry. Arjuna, if you are on the Asian continent, also works well.

To increase the blood flow make a tea or infusion of strong ginger. Take as much as a full hand of ginger, peel and slice it and put it in a large saucepan of water. Reduce the water to half and drink throughout the day.

The Diaphragm Reflex

Finally, open the diaphragm for increased capacity to be present. The diaphragm reflex is located where the elbow creases – where the radius and ulna meet. The spot will be tender and you will know when you have found it. Use the thumb to massage the reflex for several minutes each side, but do not overdo it. It is better to massage this reflex more frequently and less urgently.

Cellular Cleansing

Our cells are constantly renewing themselves. Every 27 days we have a completely different skin. Every seven years our body as a whole is completely different on a cellular level than it was seven years prior. Our bodies know how to heal and they know how to cleanse. The deeper the wound or disease however, the deeper the cleanse must be.

The genetic makeup of our tissues, fluids and bones is actually wired in from the experiences of the previous seven generations. For example, it is from the organs of the parents that many pathogens are transmitted directly to the foetus in utero. And they in turn received them from their parents. In this way the same pathogens are passed down generation after generation and we have genetic predispositions. Also, our bodily memory reaches back through the lifetimes of our mothers and grandmothers – for we were eggs in our mother's developing womb while she was in utero within our grandmother. In this way the stories and emotions of the previous generations are imprinted within us.

The body is a system of holism and reciprocity. It is an ecosystem where matter, spirit, emotion and mind are not separate. When we decide to come into our health fully, to stand in our power and/or to engage our own transformation then we will of necessity begin to cleanse. As the body sheds, the emotions will surface. The memories will come. As the spirit is touched, and the heart comes alive, the body will respond with deeper cleansing. We know we are ready to engage healing when we begin to experience sensation and emotion, or memory returns. These are indications our body gives that the cells are ready to release. When we acknowledge the wisdom of our bodies and we commit to supporting them through their innate healing capacity, we form a unity between our body, mind and spirit.

As we begin our individual processes of deeper cleansing, many shifts may occur in our personal lives. It is not uncommon to experience changes in housing, career and/or relationship. As we become 'cleaner' our sensitivity as well as our perception increases. We may find our intuition enhanced. And we will almost certainly find that we prefer different kinds of situations than we did before.

I once said to a friend, 'What will we do when the air is too dirty to breathe and the water too dirty to drink?'. She replied, 'What do you mean when?'. We live each day with skies so brown that we cannot see the Sun. We live each day with water that has become saturated with pharmaceuticals, through the waste of the billions of people prescribed and taking them each day. We live with fish that are poisonous to eat. And we live with heavy damage to our blood by processed foods and diets high in sugar and saturated fats. Our need to clean and purify the flesh is greater at this moment than ever before. Thus we are finding increasingly that diet is an incredibly powerful tool of transformation.

Diet fads have been popular for the last few decades. Recent fads include the ketosis diet and the celery juice cleanse. People report varying success with both. For myself and many that I know, however, we have had to find a diet that works just for us. Due to the increasing movement of globalism which separates us from the land of our ancestors, our intestinal flora has not yet settled, in many cases, to the places we embody. This is a process that can take many generations. And when we add engineered, undigestible food to our diet, on top of pollution as well, the body simply responds in the best ways it can. As the body copes with the multiple stressors, dis-ease will often take root in the weakest part of the system. So the individual must find the solution that responds to where the roots set down in their particular body.

Diet

In general, it is good to have a calming diet. Not too much acid, not too much sugar, not too much salt or saturated fat[2]. Beyond that you can avoid all the known allergens: wheat, corn, soy, dairy, nuts. Many people find that removing grains completely from their diet greatly improves their health. And for others, removing all forms of sugar becomes important, at least for a period of time. Follow your body's lead. If you listen, it will communicate and give feedback about what is working well and what is not.

In addition to eating a calming diet, it is helpful to eat what is growing right where you are. This food will be full of all the natural microbiomes of your area. Theses microbiomes are adapted to the bacteria and fauna that you interact with every day. This adaptation then transfers to you, strengthening your body's ability to respond to its environment. Eating local, shopping local, we create symbiosis with the Earth and the people around us which nourishes us doubly and which enlivens our immune systems. Further, if we put our hands into the earth and grow some of our food ourselves, we strengthen our body's' connection to our current microbial environment. The short- and long-term benefits of this connection cannot be underestimated.

Diet is a foundational piece to health and immunity. Upon this foundation we place our cleansing practices with breath, water, smudging, massage and movement. In addition to these approaches, we may add a focus on the spiritual heart.

The Incorruptible Seed

There lies within each one of us a seed of love and light that is incorruptible. It is the very essence of existence. And it cannot be harmed. It cannot be tarnished. It cannot be broken, lost or stolen. It is the essence of love, the heart of creation. Rumi writes of the soul of the soul of the soul. This seed, this love, is what desired to know life and to which life responds.

Earth is a plane of duality. When we accept existence as it is, we are able to tame that which is within each one of us. Only then are we able to feel the depth of our desire to know love, to know God. And from this desire, freedom

---

2 The sattvic, or calming diet, in Ayurvedic teachings is vegetarian, full of warm, cooked light foods. It encourages mental calmness. However many people find that bone broth and some light meat in small amounts actually helps them to heal. Sometimes the body needs deeper nutrition. It is all about our personal context. If you have been eating meat regularly for years, you might try giving your body a break and see what happens.

is born. From this desire, this longing for belonging, we gather courage for our journey home. Home to the heart of creation. Home to the soul of the soul of the soul. Rumi writes:

I once had a thousand desires, but in my one desire to know you all else melted away. The pure essence of your being has taken over my heart and soul. Now there is no second or third, only the sound of your sweet cry. Through your grace I have found a treasure within myself. I have found the truth of the Unseen world. I have come upon the eternal ecstasy. I have gone beyond the ravages of time. I have become one with you! Now my heart sings, I am the soul of the world.

Mantra

A very good tool for taming the mind, for bringing the heart back to its focus, is the use of mantra. Most of the major spiritual traditions have a mantra practice of some sort. The Hindu tradition has thousands of mantras for instance, each for particular qualities that need addressing. The qualities are represented as Goddesses and Gods. The Goddesses and Gods are the transmuted, pure and holy aspect of those same qualities which they tame or destroy[3]. In Sufism and Islam mantra is made from the 99 names of God. These 99 names stand for an infinite number of qualities that may express within us. All of them are God, because they exist. And because God is the incorruptible seed within each one of us, then all of creation is enfolded in that great protection, that great forgiveness and that great love. Every quality can be transformed in the heart of love[4]. And every good virtue may be increased. One way to do this is through mantra. Likewise, Christianity has in its remaining practices the use of the rosary and the Lord's Prayer. So whichever tradition or set of practices you use, the important thing is to choose one. And then follow it to the source.

---

3 Two mantras recommended for our period of collective transition are The Gayatri Mantra and Lokah Samastah Sukhino Bhavantu. These have correct pronunciation and deeper unfolding levels of meaning than we typically find on the internet. For this reason I suggest finding a community to practice with. But if you can only practice alone, do not be discouraged! The intention of your heart will open up the practice.

4 The chanting of the names of God in Sufism is known as *dhikr*. There are many groups around the world, in every location. It is good to practice with a group. If you would like support, I offer courses and introductions. You may be in contact, but it's good to connect with people where you are as well.

Prayer

Prayer is one of the most efficacious tools we have for strengthening our faith. Prayer, in its purest form, is simply silence with God. Communion. Many people use prayer as a petition, to ask for things they need or for certain outcomes in their life or in the world. This is not entirely wrong. We have needs in this life. And it is beautiful to wish for love, harmony and success for ourselves and our families. When we are able to transcend individual needs, and to pray for these things for the collective, then our prayer strengthens. And so does our faith. Our closeness with God becomes more intimate. And when we let go of desire for ourselves at ever deepening turns, the need to pray for anything specific slowly subsides. We are then able to melt into divine will. In all the ways we may pray, at all phases of our life and development, we are strengthening our skill and faith. And faith can move mountains.

Poetry and Music

Poetry and music nourish the incorruptible seed. They are like water to the seed of life and light within us. For they bypass the mind and open a direct corridor for our longings. The science of music in the East is detailed and vast. There are sounds for every moment of the day, sounds for every tiny part of the body, sounds for every mental and emotional condition. The application of sound as cure is well known. To be a master of music is to be a master healer, they are one and the same. And with indigenous peoples worldwide, the principle of music and sound as cure is known. The songs form the heritage, not as a folkloric curiosity, but as a doctor's kit for the needs of the community and tribe. Hazrat Inayat Khan writes that the soul makes its progressions through the soundscape of music. And the ancient Celtic peoples understood the same concept as soundscape and landscape. Each morning they, like the peoples of India, would rise and sing the sun into the sky. Rumi writes, 'Today you wake up sad and discouraged like any other day. Don't go into the study, pick up a musical instrument!'.

From the indigenous Americas, we also have the practice of the vision quest. And in all traditions, lengthy intensive cleansing programmes exist to help us overcome that which is within us, to bring us home to love.

Touching the Womb

Finally, we must attend to the womb. As women we often need reminders to care for ourselves. Because life depends on our care in order to continue, putting others before ourselves is an instinct. Like all instincts, it is good and useful, and we can choose how to engage it. For the truth is that if we do not care for ourselves, the life which may be dependent on us does not get cared for either. Women, men, all of us who give with empathy and selflessness – it is good for us to touch the womb. In this way we remember that the source of life needs nourishment and attention. In this way we affirm that life is worth attending to, and we remember our mother Earth, and the need for her balance.

In touching the womb we want to give more than we take. The state of the world is really a result of taking more than we give, of taking without gratitude. We can reverse this just by changing the way we focus. If we need more timber for instance, we can plant more trees. If we need more game to feed ourselves then we can cultivate the herd, and give them habitat. If we need more rest, more play and less stress, then we can create structures which put health at the top and have no tolerance for greed. When we touch the womb we remember these things.

It is the bleeding of women that reminds us all to purify. It is the sacrifice of childbirth that reminds us to surrender even our bodies to love. If women are not healthy, we are not healthy. So this healing is for all. If you do not have a womb, you may touch the womb space and tune into the womb of the mother who carried you.

Touching the Womb

You may read through this exercise and then do the exercise from memory. Or you might record yourself reading the instructions on a voice memo to play back. It's good to hear yourself speak.

- Clear and tidy your space. Light a candle. Burn an incense. You may play soft music, of waterfalls or rain. Make sure you are warm enough and get into a comfortable position. You may lie down for this one.
- Breathe in deeply, fill the torso. Breathe out fully, deflate the lungs. Allow the breathing to soften and drop your weight into the sofa, bed or cushion. Feel the support of the surface against your bones. Release a little more. Allow the weight of your arms, legs, neck, shoulders and head to fully let go. Imagine that you are floating in a pool of warm sunlight. Become luminous and relax deeper into your sense of safety.
- Allow the mind to relax. Be patient while it stills. And offer yourself endless compassion. Thank your body for carrying you. Thank your body for carrying life. Thank your mother for birthing you. Feel your commitment to your body and your self. Allow this feeling to strengthen.

- When you are ready, bring your hands to your womb. If you do not have a womb, still bring your hands to the area where a womb would be. Notice any feelings that arise. Gently be with them as your feelings rise and fall. Watch them ebb and flow like a tide. Release them as soon as they arise.
- As the tide stills, deepen your soft connection with your womb. Touch her a little more tenderly. Focus your intention to meet her, with softness. If you do not have a womb, or you are doing this exercise for a repeated time, focus your intention to meet the womb of the mother you were birthed through.
- As your connection with the womb space strengthens, ever so gently ask your womb what her name is. Our wombs, they have ancient names. So if her name is in a language you don't understand that is OK. Repeat her name out loud. Allow her to awaken within you. And again, notice any emotion that arises.
- As the tides still, begin a conversation with your womb. Listen to what she has to share. Listen with compassion. Listen with grace. Listen, even, with joy. Listen as long as you like. Begin a conversation that will last a long time.
- When you are ready, let your womb know that you need to focus on other things for the moment, but that you will say hello again. Make a commitment to yourself to keep the voice of your womb alive within you. Make a commitment to care for her. And watch how your life unfolds.

Remember to Receive

In this chapter I have shared with you practices that you may do for yourself. It is important to empower ourselves on our healing journeys and in our spiritual growth. These are introductory practices, however. They will take you a good distance, and then you might also like to get some support. There are many wonderful physical and energy healers you may go to. Below are some practices you might try, that I can personally recommend. It is important to have a rapport with the individual that you see. Someone who is recommended by others, who have received good work from them, is a good starting point[5].

- Acupuncture
- Herbal Medicine

---

5 If you feel led to go deeper and enter these fields as a healer I offer a training programme where students can become certified in several of these pathways. If you are drawn, please speak to me about it.

- Ayurvedic Nutrition
- Craniosacral Therapy
- Polarity Therapy
- Neutral-Space Relaxation®
- Reiki Healing
- Holotropic Breathwork
- Body-Mind Centring
- Alexander Technique
- Feldenkrais Awareness Through Movement
- Authentic Movement
- Somatic Experiencing
- Tai Chi or Chi Kung classes

Remember to follow your heart. You don't have to be so serious and it's perfectly good to just enjoy a fun movement class or a walk on the beach. You might even do something totally new like a circus experience day! Follow what you are drawn to. Trust yourself. And where it feels true, grounded and safe, allow yourself to be held and supported by spiritual community and by a spiritual master. Take care of each other. For each one of us who is strong, we are all strong. For each one of us who is in health, we are all in health. And vice versa.

Chapter Seven
Conclusion

Know this, we have jumped out of the past already. So many are making the migration from the lower centres to the heart. As our eyes open and we let go of our traumas, gently and with compassion, we are then able to show up with more and more presence to the heart space. When that happens we gain momentum, and the choices which seemed so difficult only a little while before become effortless. It is the power of love, pouring forth from the heart, by which the new life ways are successfully built. And we can do it, because we already are. Look around you: who in your local community is aligned with this fresh vibration? What happens when you move into that circle of connection? Some call it magic but it is in truth the fruit of all the efforts, seeking and release you have already done. In this moment we don't look back. Welcome love with open arms. It is your birthright and our collective homecoming.

In this text we have covered a lot of ground, yet there is so much more that could be shared. Let us allow that sharing to happen through conversation. For in conversation our edges meet and from that fertile ground solutions arise. Divisions are formed from a rigidity of ideas, they do not stem from the heart. And to connect heart to heart, we must first enter the process of knowing ourselves. When we are each divinely aligned – and there we meet – so much power is generated. We are part of a journey through time. A magnificent journey. And we are lucky to be conscious and aware as we play our parts. Let's take care of each other. For in the heart, borders, nations and even race no longer make any sense. We are one human race. Because belief is based in the mind, it can be used to divide humans one from the other. Love, on the other hand, slowly moves us toward unity.

Coming up, the weather changes will increase. Already there are more fires and floods. Already many have lost their habitat. Already there is starvation. We will see, sooner than we may be prepared for, that food, energy and economic sovereignty are actually foundational to our survival. We are letting go at a level that many of us are only beginning to comprehend. We have known intimately the havoc of the strain we have been living under. Yet still the moment is a shock. And we as a collective have been in serious denial about the magnitude of what is needed to move through the changes we are experiencing as a species. We are facing fundamental rifts within our collective psyche. And some will handle it better than others, and better at some times more than others. We are fragile, and all in a process. When I see colleagues and families separate themselves from each other, I feel sad.

The Dalai Lama, as well as our spiritual and indigenous leaders, remind us that the problems we face are of our own creation. They urge us to joy and exemplify that joy is a state of being much deeper and more persistent than happiness (2016). For in pursuing happiness, we are closely tied to the objects or sources of its arrival. When we tune ourselves to divine joy, however, we become a living antidote for grief and its ever-present causes.

Letting go of the past does not mean that we throw all of the beauty, learning and wisdom it has given us away. Rather, it can serve to reinforce the bonds that are fundamental between us, and allow us to merge and share our knowledges for the benefit of all. There is much the developed world has to learn from the undeveloped. Ideas of poverty and wealth, sickness and health, family and kin, may merge into something of beauty for all sides.

Each one of us is coming home – to ourselves, to love, to each other. As we realise how far from home we have been, the metaphysical grief begins to open. And it is good. Like rain, these tears clear the air for fresh flowing currents of joy. Like rain, these tears water the soil so that flowers and life may grow. As a species we are moving rapidly through the emotional history of the 20th century, and possibly even deeper time. As we expand into the fifth world, our cellular memory opens for release. We experience the fear, doubt, anger, shame and grief we have endured. Of all that we have done to each other. And as we do so, it shifts. We feel the emotions as they are leaving. And nothing that is happening to catalyse our release is an accident. Despite apparent woes, there is a divine unfolding taking place.

It is not an accident that in 1984 a white buffalo calf was born in Wyoming, the United States. The 1980s through the 2020s has been recognised at a gateway period between the ages, astrologically as well as spiritually. It is an end as well as a beginning and we may find that the human capacity for change, once ignited, is incredible. As we shift out of the present age, we may give ourselves permission to expand our imaginations beyond current paradigms. Not only are civilisation and lifestyle changing, but also the way we engage the sacred and religion, technology and communications.

The Heart

It may indeed be that a lot of what we see happening around us is serving a healthy purpose. It may be that all of our darkness needs to be seen and acknowledged before we can move on. It may be that an evolution towards peace is only possible through clear-seeing and open eyes. As humans we project what is within us outward. Seeing it outside of ourselves, we are then able to attend and deal with it more easily.

We are in a river which is always flowing towards the ocean. And the ocean is an ocean of love. It cannot be anything else. We come from love, and to love we return, and in the journey we learn how to sense, feel and act through love.

Vibration, instinct and intuition are navigation tools as we open our sails. Vibration does not lie, but it does not always match our intellect or mind. To sense, feel and act from the heart requires eyes that are wide open.

Our bodies are not separate from spirit. When our soul takes its flight, the body may remain on the Earth, but while we are here the body and spirit are one. The particles and atoms of our flesh become the soil, plants and air. The water of our bodies becomes the water of the Earth. To ensure life for the coming generations, we must attend with love to all levels of our existence. One type of sovereignty does not exist without the other.

For some, hope and beauty will be easy. For others, there will be a process. No matter how diabolical the energies are that are coming up to be cleansed, you are safe and stable in the centre of love. Love wins.

To do your best is enough. When your arrows are focused in one direction, commitment and inspiration are natural. If we are living without joy, this is an indication that we need to create or accept change for our lives. Rumi writes, 'Do not ask what love can make or do – look at the colours of the world!'.

As we see the depths of the depths that we are capable of, and the heights of the heights that we may soar to, we may choose to remain in the centre. From a neutral position, we are less distracted by either shadow or light. In this way we remain free to soar in the endless bliss of emptiness and peace.

Peace may feel different than we are accustomed to. After hundreds of years of speeding up, pushing and ignoring our inner instincts, it may take time to re-conceptualise equilibrium enough to live it. Humility at the magnitude of our task, and compassion for the vessel of our form will lead us to the still waters of peace. In the middle of the ocean, there is endless stillness. There are endless stars. The horizon of potentiality stretches out in all directions. Feelings like this, close to omnipresence, may take some time to get used to.

Grounding is important as we open. So are self love and self care. Cultivating our soil and pruning our stems through daily practice encourages our flowering and resilience.

In the end, it is more helpful to us if we move beyond ideas of good and bad. Everything has a divine purpose. And we are, knowingly and unknowingly, releasing the energies and ideas that no longer serve humanity and the planet. Joy is our new foundation. Our children deserve, at the very least, our joy for their courageous arrival. It is seeds of joy and peace that will nourish the next seven generations.

A Prayer

In this moment Great Spirit, I am grateful we are allowing ourselves to unravel. I am grateful we are seeing what no longer serves us. I am grateful for sickness and for health, for understanding I don't need to work so hard. I am grateful to slow down, to learn, to love myself. I am grateful that life is enough, and I release my need for material belongings. I am grateful for beauty, harmony and light. I am grateful for clean water, food and beautiful companions. Thank you. The birds are singing. The stars are shining. My children are happy. And right now I truly see that we are one human family. May these good things grow, and may the new world being born within us be bright, joyful and clean. May we have resilience as we move through time. And may the breath and sun which sustain us ever shine. For our health, liberation and peace we give thanks. (July 2020)

No Death

To remember our purpose here, why we came, is to remember the simplicity of love. We are beings of love. Our bodies are made of light. It is to love that we return, and that is why we are here, to make the journey. In truth, there is no death. We simply change clothes as we move from one form to another. The dimensions beyond are infinite. And it is up to each one of us where we sojourn and for how long. It is up to the interplay, the relationship, between ourselves and God. Let's remember that God is not a bad word. Nor is prayer. Or purity. These are realities of existence. And no church, no corporation truly has the power to distort that which is. The eternal unfolding of God, that which is love, does not mind which names we use or which path we follow to return home. The essential unity moves across traditions, across religions.

As we slow down we have an opportunity to change track. While we face our fears of death, significant spaces are opening within us. If we can stay slow, stay in the presence, we will have all doors open. Now is the moment of our migration. And we don't want to miss it, running about. When the doors to our next world swing wide for us, we should be ready to enter them. And to have the stamina for that journey it is good and important to care for our psycho-spiritual-body. For dust returns to dust, and spirit returns to spirit.

As we move through the Earth's changes and the epochs of time, we might still make an upward journey out of an age of darkness.

Stay awake. Don't go back to sleep.
The breezes at dawn have secrets to tell you.
The door is round and open.
People are moving across the sill
where the two worlds meet.
You must ask for what you really want.
Mevlana Jalaluddin Rumi

Bibliography

Bader, John C. 2019. 'If every 8 year old in the world is taught meditation, we will eliminate violence in the world in one generation', In *The Responsive Universe*. Available at https://responsiveuniverse.me/2012/11/20/if-every-8-year-old-in-the-world-is-taught-meditation-we-will-eliminate-violence-from-the-world-within-one-generation-dalai-lama/. Accessed 30 October 2021.

Banyacya, Thomas. 1995. 'Hopi Prophecy' at the *Whole Life Expo*, Las Vegas. Public Talk. Available at https://www.youtube.com/watch?v=qfFJFgnmJdE. Sacred Land Film Project. 31 March 2020. Accessed 4 October 2021.

Braidotti, Rosi. 2011. *Nomadic Subjects: Embodiment and Sexual Difference in Contemporary Feminist Theory*. Columbia University Press.

Cameron, Anne. 1981. *Daughters of Copper Woman*. Press Gang Publishers.

Chan, Victor. 2010. Western women can come to the rescue of the world'. The Dalai Lama Centre. Available online at https://dalailamacenter.org/blog-post/western-women-can-come-rescue-world Accessed 3 October 2021.

Chitty, John and Muller, Mary Louise. 1990. *Energy Exercises: Easy Exercises for Health and Vitality.'* Polarity Press.

Chomsky, Noam and Prashad, Vijay. 2021a. 5 January. Chomsky and Prashad: There are 3 major threats to life on Earth that we must address in 2021. *Alternet*. Available at https://chomsky.info/20210105/. Accessed 25 October 2021.

Chomsky, Noam and Pollin, Robert. 2021b. 16 August. *Chomsky and Pollin: We Can't Rely on Private Sector for Necessary Climate Action*. Available at https://chomsky.info/20210816/. Accessed 25 October 2021.

Chomsky, Noam and Horvat, Srecko. 2020. 28 March. Noam Chomsky: Coronavirus – what is at stake? *DiEM25 TV*. Available at https://youtu.be/t-N3ln2rLl4. Accessed 25 October 2021.

Clow, Barbara Hand. 2007. *The Mayan Code*. Bear & Company.

Dalai Llama, The and Tutu, Desmond with Abrams, Douglas. 2016. *The Book of Joy*. Hutchinson.

Davies, Caleb. 2021. Why future homes could be made of living fungus. In *The EU Research and Innovation Magazine*. Available at https://phys.org/news/2021-01-future-homes-fungus.html. Accessed 3 October 2021.

Eisenstein, Charles. 2020. *The Coronation*. Available at https://charleseisenstein.org/essays/the-coronation/. Accessed 3 October 2021.

Elders of the Hopi Nation. 2000. Oraibi, Arizona, 8 June. *We are the ones.* Public talk. Available at https://artistic.umn.edu/we-are-ones-weve-been-waiting-prophecy-made-hopi-elders. University of Minnesota. 23 July 2020. 'Artistic Antidote for a Pandemic'. Accessed 3 October 2021.

Elders of the Lakota Nation. 2019. *Life Lakota: The Cheyenne River Reservation.* Film. Vativ Media. Available at https://youtu.be/nbSRUtuWh7s. Accessed 3 October 2021.

Event 201. 2019. *Public-private Cooperation for Pandemic Preparedness and Response.* Available at https://www.centerforhealthsecurity.org/event201/recommendations.html. Accessed 3 October 2021.

Firstenburg, Arthur. 2020. *The Invisible Rainbow: A History of Electricity and Life.* Chelsea Green Publishing.

Friedlander, Shems. 2003. (Original 1975.) *Rumi and the Whirling Dervishes.* Archetype.

Guenon, Rene. 2009. (Original 1927.) Introduction to the reign of quantity and the signs of the times. In *The Essential Rene Guenon: Metaphysics, Tradition and the Crisis of Modernity*, pp. 43–62. World Wisdom.

Gupta, Sunetra. 2021. All I'm presenting is a range of possibilities. In *The Biologist.* Royal Society of Biology. Available at https://www.rsb.org.uk/biologist-covid-19/sunetra-gupta-interview-2. Accessed 3 October 2021.

Hafiz (trans. Ladinsky, Daniel). 1999. *The Gift.* Compass Books.

Hall, Claire Louise. 2007. *Outside the Skies Are Crying for Me.* Unpublished song.

Hoskins, Liz. 2017. Learning from Nature's laws and lore. In *Resurgence & Ecologist*, Sep/Oct, No. 304.

Khan, Hazrat Inayat. 2005. *The Music of Life.* Omega. First published 1983.

Khan, Hazrat Inyat. 1996. *The Mysticism of Sound and Music: The Teaching of Hazrat Ina-yat Khan*, Dragon edition, p. 127–128. Shambhala.

Kunuk, Zacharias. 2001. *The Fast Runner* (Film). Isuma Igloolik Production.

Looking Horse, Chief Arvol. 2010. 27 August. *Chief Arvol Looking Horse Speaks of White Buffalo Prophecy.* KnewWays. Available at https://youtu.be/PHqVdZmpRgI. Accessed 2 November 2021.

Looking Horse, Chief Arvol. 2021. 29 June. *Special World Peace and Prayer Day Message – Chief Arvol Looking Horse and Friends.* WE Campaign. Live Talk. Available at https://youtu.be/YtFOMwmxDxU. Accessed 31 October 2021.

Masayesva, Vernon with Shirato, Tetsu. 2020. 6 September. *Hopi – Messages from the Ancients.* Film. Available at https://youtu.be/Xn65fJp6m8A. Accessed 31 October 2021.

Moon, Sheila. 1984. *Changing Woman and Her Sisters.* Guild for Psychological Studies.

Moss, Robert. 2005. *Dreamways of the Iroquois: Honouring the Secret Wishes of the Soul.* Destiny Books, pp. 108–109, 114–130.

Mumford, Elaine. 2016. Growing up green in Rajasthan: Feminism and grassroots desertification combat in Piplantri village. In *Yale Review of International Studies*, Feb. Available at http://yris.yira.org/essays/1639. Accessed 3 October 2021.

Myss, Caroline. 1996. *Anatomy of the Spirit: The Seven Stages of of Power and Healing*. Three Rivers Press.

Obomsawin, Alanis. *Alanis Obomsawin* in Quotes: The Web's Largest Resource for Quotes and Sayings. Available at https://www.quotes.net/authors/Alanis+Obomsawin. Accessed 3 October 21.

Pirsig, Robert. 1991.'*Zen and the Art of Motorcycle Maintenance: An Inquiry into Value*'. Vintage Classics.

Rapid Transition Alliance. 2019. *Transition Towns – the quiet, networked revolution*. Available at https://www.rapidtransition.org/stories/transition-towns-the-quiet-networked-revolution/. Accessed 3 October 21.

Rumi, Mevlana Jalaluddin. *The Mathnavi*. Multiple dates. Multiple translators, including Nicholson, Reynolds; Arberry J.J.; Barks, Coleman; Maby, Juliet.

Schuon, Frithjof. 1984. *The Transcendent Unity of Religions*. Fons Vitae.

Schafer, Karen with White Eagle. 2021. 2 June. *Channelled message*. Available at http://www.whiteeaglespeaks.net/home/TodaysMessage.aspx. Accessed 31 October 2021.

Shiva, Vandana. 1988. *Staying Alive: Women, Ecology and Development*. Zed Books.

Shiva, Vandana. 2016. *Who Really Feeds The World?*, pp. 52–53. Zed Books.

Stone, Dr Randolph. 1986a. *Polarity Therapy: The Complete Collected Works*. Volume 1. CRCS Publications.

Stone, Dr Randolph. 1986b. *Polarity Therapy: The Complete Collected Works*. Volume 2. CRCS Publications.

Tutu, Desmond and Allen, John. 2013. 26 March. *Desmond Tutu, Peacemaker: A conversation with Desmond Tutu and John Allen*. Pepperdine University. Available at https://youtu.be/hOaSbGD7Was. Accessed 31 October 2021.

Tutu, Desmond and Tutu, Mpho. 2014. *The Book of Forgiving: The Fourfold Path for Heal-ing Ourselves and the World*. William Collins.

Tweedie, Irina. 2014. *Daughter of Fire: A Diary of a Spiritual Training with a Sufi Master'*. The Golden Sufi Centre Publishing.

United Nations. 1992. *United Nations Conference on Environment & Development Rio de Janeiro, Brazil*, 3–14 June 1992. United Nations Sustainable Development. Available at https://sustainabledevelopment.un.org/content/documents/Agenda21.pdf. Accessed 3 October 21.

Villoldo, Alberto. 2010. *Illumination: The Shaman's Way of Healing*. Hay House.

Vitale, Joe. 2009. *Zero Limits: The Secret Hawaiian System for Wealth, Health, Peace and More*. John Wiley and Sons.

Yogananda, Paramahansa. 2007. *Autobiography of a Yogi*. Self Realization Fellowship. First published 1946.

Yukteswar, Sri Giri. 1949. *The Holy Science*. Public Domain. Originally published 1894.

Westerman, Floyd Red Crow. 2008. *Tribute to Floyd Red Crow Westerman*. Native Voice TV. Available at https://youtu.be/OyARwbwAeyI. Accessed 2 November 2021.

Index

Index

Index